Assertively Managing "Difficult" People

Andrew D. Pope

The right of Andrew D. Pope to be identified as the author of this work has been asserted by him in accordance with the Copyright, Designs and Patents Act, 1988

Copyright © 2016 Andrew D. Pope

All rights reserved. No part of this publication may be reproduced, stored in retrieval system or transmitted in any form or by any means electronic, mechanical, photocopying, recording or otherwise, without the prior permission of the author and publisher, except in the case of brief quotations embodied in critical articles and reviews.

Copyright © 2016 Andrew D. Pope

All rights reserved.

ISBN: 9781521494585

DEDICATION

To my wonderful wife Julie

CONTENTS

	Preface	i
1	The results you will get from following this guide	1
2	Your recipe for success	5
3	Your journey begins here	9
4	What constitutes a "difficult" person?	14
5	What exactly is this assertiveness thing?	19
6	Start as you mean to go on	25
7	Protect yourself so you can help and protect others	32
8	The hostile-aggressive influencing style	37
9	The hostile-manipulative influencing style	48
10	The passive influencing style	79
11	The workplace psychopath	92
12	Modelling excellence and learning from others	107
13	Summary and your next steps	110
	Legal notice and general disclaimer	113

PREFACE

Learn how to manage difficult personality types with confidence and assertiveness

Managing the difficult personality types at work can be something of a nightmare for many line managers and supervisors. Some managers seem to have the amazing knack of effectively and confidently with the difficult personality types they encounter. Even if you are a relatively inexperienced manager or supervisor right now this short practical no-nonsense guide will help you on your way to becoming the effective and dynamic leader of your staff you really want to be.

Part of the "The New Manager's Survive & Thrive Guides" series.

Chapter 1

The results you will get from following this guide

We encounter "difficult" people every day. Now I am sure we all want to keep our cool under pressure, right? These people however are stressful to us and they can ruin our day in a heartbeat. We avoid them whenever we can, am I right?

These difficult people are the ones who exhibit behaviours, communication styles and influencing styles which can wreak havoc with your life, the lives of your staff and which can even affect the success of whole organisations depending on the position they are in.

It can be bad enough working with or being around such people but what about actually managing them?

Some managers, however, seem to have the amazing knack of effectively and confidently dealing with the difficult and problematic personality types they encounter. Whether they get them back on side, neutralise them in some way or even forcibly eject them these managers appear to cope with almost magical ease. Would you like to be able to cope in a similar manner? If they can do it, why not you?

Of course, managing some difficult personalities can terrify even the most confident and experienced managers and supervisors. Is it not often easier just to bypass them and hope someone else does the work? Anything for a quiet life right? No, not really.

Sometimes the stakes are high. You are the manager and you need to manage. What if you lack experience and confidence as a manager or supervisor and your position depends on getting these difficult people to perform and grow or join with the team and do their share of the work? The stress can build. Do you lie awake at night dreading your next day at work? What do you do to turn this situation around?

Are you a newly promoted manager or supervisor? Have you ever had to directly deal with such difficult people yourself? You want to do a good job but do you know the best ways to handle difficult staff?

You also have to manage your own position within the organisation so care must be taken to work effectively within the organisational constraints of policy, politics and hierarchy.

Have you been in your management position for a short while yet still feel you lack the practical skills and experience to deal effectively with these difficult types? Do not let them hold you back.

You might even have been a manager for a while yet you still worry about the right way to go about it. You are not alone. We all have our strong areas and we all have areas we could improve on.

If any of the above applies to you then you should definitely be reading and acting on the contents of this guide. It is part of a whole series aimed squarely at new, inexperienced or keen to improve managers and supervisors.

Amongst other things, by the end of this guide:

- You will understand why some people are considered more difficult to work with than others
- You will find out more about the often mentioned but seldom explained concept of assertiveness and how to be an assertive manager
- You will learn to identify the influencing styles of three main difficult personality types
- You will take away lots of practical transferable tools and techniques to deal with some specific examples of the more aggressive, passive-aggressive and passive personalities
- You will get a practical and super-effective strategy to help you plan for your success when starting to use these tools and techniques
- You will be a lot more confident and happy in your new managerial or supervisory role and the people around you will see and appreciate the many positive changes.

In case you are wondering who this Andrew D. Pope character is, please allow me to introduce myself.

I am an author, trainer and emotional intelligence coach. I am based in South Wales in the UK. Everything I do in my life and work is about helping people with emotional resilience, life balance and effective interpersonal communication.

Life is always a work in progress and we all need a helping hand once in a while.

Developing your options and your abilities to communicate effectively with your staff and teams will give you real confidence and you will be well on your way to managerial excellence.

Chapter 2

Your recipe for success

You will get the warts and all theory and practical information you will need to first understand and then to more confidently manage and deal with a wide variety of difficult personality types at work and in everyday life. You will start to build the confidence to spread your wings and become a far better manager.

You will study the much talked about but often poorly understood trait of assertiveness and how to develop it as a manager or supervisor when dealing with difficult staff.

All interpersonal or "soft" skills come under the umbrella term of Emotional Intelligence or EI. Assertiveness is very definitely part of your emotional intelligence toolkit. You may well have heard of this term and in my work I deal with all aspects of EI and assist people to develop more of it and apply it more in their everyday lives. The skills have been around for many years but the term was popularised by Daniel Goleman in his book of the same name.

EI breaks down into four main areas which I call the 4Us:

- Understanding what makes us tick
- Usefully regulating our own behaviour
- Understanding what makes others tick
- Using our knowledge to build and maintain relationships with others

This guide will certainly help you develop your ability to manage the third and fourth U. Note that a high and well-balanced level of EI is seen as being an extremely valuable trait to possess in modern business. I will refer to EI more when covering each of the "difficult" types.

We are going to focus on the personality types who can and do cause huge issues with their influencing style and associated interpersonal behaviours. In my experience and, more importantly, in the experience of many of my coaching clients, these type of situations are amongst the most common and can create many problematic situations for managers and supervisors as well as other staff.

Learning and applying new or better ways of managing and dealing with these people will make you a better and happier manager all round.

Each chapter builds your knowledge and also features "Action points" to encourage you to take a practical and proactive approach to asking yourself some tough searching questions and trying out the techniques and ideas. Live practice and solid feedback are the only ways to really get good at something.

As you will no doubt have noticed, I have made a deliberate and specific decision to make sure this book is laser-focused and flab free. I appreciate your valuable time is at a premium so with this in mind I am making my books only as long as they absolutely need to be to get the message out there and doing good things.

My business coaching clients all benefit from short intense sessions so I have chosen to create my "The New Manager's Survive & Thrive Guides" series to replicate this short yet intense experience in book form.

Each book in the series is self-contained and each fully delivers on its promise. They are all effectively equivalent to three or four hours of intensive one to one coaching with me distilled into the written word. The series as a whole will aim to offer a comprehensive system of learning for the avid reader.

All the books in the series are aimed primarily at newly promoted or novice managers and supervisors. In my experience, whenever any expert or technical worker gets promoted to a management or supervisory role they almost always encounter a number of commonly recurring problems relating to their interpersonal and communication skills. There are also real world organisational factors of politics and vested interest to negotiate. The end results are worth it but it is not always a smooth road.

Managing other people is a skillset many newly promoted people are assumed to automatically possess. Alas, most new managers and supervisors do not have these skills and do not even know where to begin to learn them. Left to their own devices they have a miserable time as a new manager and they can also create huge amounts of chaos and misery for those around them into the bargain.

Again in my experience, time is of the essence so they always seek to find an accessible, practical and no-nonsense solution to their particular problem and this is where my books fit in.

My "The New Manager's Survive & Thrive Guides" series will provide a growing number of short sharp and right to the point guides specifically focused on areas of management and leadership which new managers, new supervisors or new team leaders can use again and again whenever they feel the need.

I hope you enjoy and benefit from this particular volume in the series and, if you have not already done so, please check out and enjoy the rest.

Let us get cracking.

Chapter 3

Your journey begins here

We all want to be able to keep our cool under pressure, am I right? We all want to be the manager who can deal with everyone. We all want to be the person who negotiates smoothly through all their interpersonal interactions no matter who they are with. Of course we do, this is why you are reading this guide. So what exactly is this "keeping your cool" thing all about?

Keeping your cool simply means keeping your emotions at an appropriate level and in equilibrium; keeping them in balance. Balance is important in our lives; it certainly is in mine.

We need balance in many areas such as sleeping versus waking, group activity versus alone time, relaxing versus working, food intake versus waste excretion, etc. When we get unbalanced we generally feel out of sorts and we often do not perform at our best. Other people generally notice the negative changes too. Our working environment can generate a huge number of situations with the potential to create imbalance for us.

Most professional people spend a lot of time at work and many of us spend a lot of time interacting with and managing other people whilst we are at work. It stands to reason during these work-based and managerial interactions there will be times when we will rub people up the wrong way, they will rub us up the wrong way or we will disagree with them in some fashion. This is normal and healthy. I would be more worried if a business coaching client told me there were never any disagreements at all.

Most of these disagreements or other negative encounters are naturally quite short-lived. We have the disagreement or the full and frank discussion and the air is cleared. We reset the dials and everyone gets back to doing what they do best.

If there is a difficult person or two in the wider working environment this is not really a problem to us either. We can generally take steps to minimise contact with them whenever possible and there are often large time gaps between interactions.

This is not always the case, however, and at some point in our professional lives we have all encountered (or at least heard tell about) one or more extremely difficult personality types with whom we have had to work closely with or deal with for any extended period. It can be far worse when you are the manager and others are looking to you to handle the situation or do the right thing.

If you have ever managed a difficult person you work with closely, you may have found yourself dreading the prospect and avoiding them whenever possible. You might even have made changes to your schedule or even found yourself taking different route in and out of your building to reduce the chances of interacting with them. Your daydreams might have involved them being killed in a hideous way or maybe you have sacked them and thrown out the door; anything which gets them far away from you.

Life is not as easy as this however. The quality of your work and health can suffer, the quality of your other working relationships can suffer and you can physically and mentally suffer as a result of stress building up to unbearable levels. This happens and it can happen more than you might think.

Problems with difficult staff and co-workers can often have a knock-on effect at home too.

Your loved ones can end up bearing the brunt of your stress and frustration. Rather than acknowledge and face up to the problems you displace your emotions on others who probably will not or cannot fight back.

So, all in all, if you are a manager or supervisor and you are putting up with difficult personalities for too long in the workplace it can take a toll on your career and it often takes a toll on your health and well-being. It can also have a wider reaching negative impact on the entire company or organisation.

So, is ignoring it all and hoping it just goes away on its own a viable option?

No it is not.

Not managing the situation actually makes it far worse. You lose confidence and control. You are perceived as either a weak or lazy manager; possibly both. The people who are being difficult will simply carry on as they normally do and could even increase their level of difficult behaviour when they notice your lack of impact. The people who look to you for leadership, guidance, protection and support will probably lose respect for you and mark you down as another timeserving waste of space. Not a good place for you be and not a good outcome for your organisation as a whole.

What is the solution?

Take a stand! Simply refuse to put up with it! Deal with it! Deal with it right away!

Make the decision to manage the situation. The only way to become a good manager is to increase your practical managerial skillset whenever and wherever you are. Theory and ideas are always useful up to a point but in my experience, practical application of skills, tools and techniques is what gets the job done in the real world.

The best way to get through your managerial working day is to manage difficult people and difficult interpersonal interactions in a timely manner and with an assertive approach.

The aim of this guide is to help you do this by giving you some theory and ideas but mostly practical and actionable behavioural techniques, mental attitudes and strategic approaches for each of three generally difficult personality types you might well find at work with those broken down into fifteen more specific examples for deeper analysis.

There are of course far more examples of difficult personalities out there but this guide will get you started and you can use the transferable skills you learn to design your own assertive solutions to many if not all of the situations you may encounter.

I have also included quite a large section at the end of the guide detailing the type known as the workplace psychopath; just in case you have the misfortune to encounter such a person. Well worth a read.

You could also use the material to help other managers or supervisors if you know they are encountering similar difficulties. Make sure you send them to Amazon to buy their own copy though. We hard working authors need to put food on the table too.

Enjoy the guide and enjoy being better able to keep your cool when managing and dealing with difficult people.

Chapter 4

What constitutes a difficult person?

The simplest and most useful definition of a difficult person for this guide is someone you consistently do not interact effectively with or do not communicate well with. Sounds obvious right? It is indeed obvious but this simple definition is so often forgotten.

A more specific definition for a management guide like this would be:

A difficult person is someone who consistently exhibits behaviour which is disruptive or harmful to you, other staff, the team, the department or even the organisation as a whole.

Does this definition mean the difficult person is automatically and inherently bad in some way? Of course not. Not necessarily anyway. They may actually turn out to be just plain bad of course but it is a good approach not to assume this from the get go.

Here is a switch. They in turn may find you and your personality and behaviours difficult. Wow! I bet you had not considered this? Most people do not. We often assume we are perfect and everyone else is creating the problems. If this is what you believe then you need to think again. I am nowhere near perfect (author's note; my wife will happily confirm this) and I will bet money you are not perfect either. As a matter of fact, nobody is perfect and it is just something we have to live with.

There are so many ways people in any working environment can satisfy our disruptive or harmful behaviour definition and I cannot possibly cover all the permutations in this one book.

I have chosen therefore to focus on influencing style and associated interpersonal behaviours.

In my experience and, more importantly in the experience of many of my coaching clients, influencing style issues can cause the most grief for managers and supervisors as well as other staff. Learning to identify and then applying new or better ways of managing and dealing with these styles will make you a better, more effective and generally happier manager.

Modern life is all about influence. We are influencing and being influenced all the time. Sometimes consciously or deliberately and sometimes subconsciously or accidentally.

You interact with and try to influence others using something called your preferred influencing style. You will find out exactly what the styles are in the next chapter.

You can now consider "difficult" people as being those with an influencing style markedly different to your own.

This is the perspective I will take in this particular book and a better understanding of influencing styles will serve you well in your dealings with everyone you interact with. Often it only takes some simple understanding and small changes to make a world of difference in how you interact with these people.

There are, however, people who are far more extreme in their influencing style "difficulty" level and they often cause problems for the majority of the people they interact with. Many of these types are common enough or so problematic they deserve their own unique classifications and names; at least on an informal basis. Some types are covert and some are out in the open.

Note many people can and do exhibit different types or combinations of "difficult" behaviour either consistently or at different times and in different contexts/scenarios. Real life is never as clear cut or obvious as we would like it to be.

As a manager or supervisor you will often have to first identify and then deal with many of these extreme types so this guide focuses right in on them.

Here is the bottom line. If we are honest, we are all ultimately looking to change problem situations and our responses to them in order to keep our cool. Now this goal may initially lead us to think a key strategy would be to change the other person in some way. Wrong! Here is an incredibly important point to bear in mind as we progress. Tempting as it is to try, you cannot actually change anyone else. They alone can make the choice to change and not you. You can help them if they ask for help but until then they are on their own. The key thing to note is you can change your own mindsets and attitudes to other people and you can definitely change your communication and behavioural responses towards them and their behaviour.

We are all part of wider systems and many of these systems overlap. If you change your response to anything it will have an impact on the systems surrounding you. This means you may well enable or encourage others to change themselves as an indirect result of your impact on a system of which you are both a part and I will refer back to this point several times in this mini-guide.

In any interaction with other people we have choices we can make. We can choose how to respond. Even in stressful situations which flood our bodies with adrenalin and cortisol and trigger our "fight or flight" response, once the initial reaction ends we then choose how to respond next. I always use the example of road rage. After the initial fright of a close call is over, if you start to chase after the perpetrator to enact some sort of revenge tactic it is because you have chosen to maintain the anger and desire for revenge. You can also choose not to do it.

What you will learn in this guide is how to calmly and deliberately consider how you will response to the situations created when you and a difficult person interact. You will assertively deal with or take away the difficult element in the scenario and therefore keep your cool. This may well educate the other person to deal with you differently next time or even prompt them to make their own changes in how they deal with other people as well but, and here is the thing, if this happens it will be because they chose to do it.

To be a better manager, you simply have to choose to keep your cool and remain assertive throughout. Sounds like a fair deal to me.

By the way, in case you thought this is a guru-inspired easy ride, there are no short cuts and it may well be hard work at times. I never make false claims or promises.

If something is worth doing it is worth putting some effort into it and doing it well.

Chapter Action Points

This action point involves some thinking and prioritising the influencing styles of your team or those around you at work.

How many people are in your team, department or work unit?

How many of these people would you describe as difficult to get along with or manage in terms of their influencing style and interpersonal behaviours?

How many would you class as easy to get along with and manage?

What are the key difference do you think?

If you had to prioritise the difficult characters, which one would you like to deal with first and why?

Keep going with your list and prioritise the rest.

Keep the list safe because you will refer back to it several times before the end of the book.

Chapter 5

What exactly is this assertiveness thing?

Assertiveness is one of those things everyone has heard about but no-one can easily define. We are often told to be more assertive but what exactly is it we are supposed to do more of? How assertive are we right now?

Your level of assertiveness and comfort when being assertive can have a big effect on your overall management and leadership style so this stuff is important.

There are many on-line self-evaluation questionnaires available so if you want to find out your current level of assertiveness or your preferred interpersonal or influencing style then feel free to try them out. As with most things in life, there can be good or bad and free or paid for; take your pick.

There are four main classifications of influencing style of which assertiveness is but one:

- Assertive
- Passive
- Hostile-aggressive
- Manipulative-aggressive (aka passive-aggressive)

Assertive is what we are aiming for so more on this a bit later.

Passive is a type characterised by an "I must lose and you must win" attitude.

Hostile-aggressive is an influencing style characterised by an "I must win and you must lose" mentality.

The last influencing style listed is termed manipulative-aggressive or passive-aggressive and this type is characterised by an "I must lose so you must lose" mindset.

All of these styles are on a continuum and we all exhibit the different traits in different degrees at various times in our lives. People are not so clearly defined. Over the long-term it is likely we will favour one style over the others. Even if you are not sure, ask your trusted colleagues and they will tell you what style they think you prefer and exhibit most. It may shock you.

By and large, most of us choose to adopt the passive stance whenever possible, especially at work. You know the old "anything for a quiet life" and "why rock the boat" approach. Does the saying, "If it ain't broke, don't fix it" sound familiar?

If you are going to be a better manager then you need to be as assertive as possible. You therefore need to know what assertiveness actually is so I had better start by defining it.

For our purposes I am sure we can all reasonably agree assertiveness involves being completely clear and open about how one feels, what one needs and how it can be fairly achieved. This requires assertive communication skills, assertive body language, confidence and the ability to communicate calmly without attacking or yielding unnecessarily to another person.

A definition of the word assert is to state a fact or belief confidently and forcefully. You are going to learn to calmly tell it like it is in order to control the difficult person whilst protecting yourself and the rest of your team. It is the way of the effective manager.

Assertive people understand and believe they have a number of rights and an expectation to certain things and ways of being treated in their work. These rights and expectations come with a responsibility to accord other people the same rights and expectations. So this idea of assertiveness adheres to a win-win approach to life. Adopt an "I get what I want and you get what you want" approach and everyone is generally happy.

Sounds simple so why are we not all doing more of it?

We should be, because learning to be more assertive will help us to express our thoughts and feelings freely, speak up and defend ourselves, know and stand up for our rights, negotiate reasonably and control our emotions effectively during periods of interpersonal conflict.

Difficult people do not generally follow a win-win approach themselves. Some are difficult unwittingly and some are difficult knowingly. As a manager or leader you have to be assertive for yourself and on behalf of your team. They look to you for support and to do the right thing. Bear in mind as we go on that the difficult person who is difficult deliberately and with malice aforethought has essentially given up their right to get what they want once you have engaged assertively with the situation. You will deal with them assertively but the win-win aspect of the situation is for you and your team. In my opinion, and experience bears this out, the deliberately difficult person only has the right to be treated fairly and with respect. The decision to make suitable changes to their future behaviour rests with them alone. You always have the option to escalate things if they fail to change sufficiently.

As I mention the terms Emotional Intelligence, self-confidence, self-esteem and emotional resilience in the upcoming sections I will briefly define them here too.

Emotional Intelligence (also known as EI or EQ) can be usefully summed up as how knowledgeable we are about ourselves, how driven or self-motivated we are and what makes us tick combined with how knowledgeable we are about other people and what makes them tick and also how we interact interpersonally with those people. The ability to understand how to interact well with others can also be called social intelligence. Some people can have low self-awareness but have high social awareness and vice versa.

Self-esteem can be usefully defined here as being how we feel about ourselves at any particular point in time and self-confidence can be usefully defined here as being how confident we are feeling about using our skills and knowledge.

Emotional resilience can be usefully defined here as the ability to experience negative emotional impacts yet bounce back stronger than ever.

I know it is a bit of a shameless sales pitch but you might consider buying and reading another of books. It is called The Resilient Professional. The Resilient Professional has a host of practical tips and strategies for boosting confidence, increasing emotional resilience and re-interpreting success and failure through appropriate feedback and self-talk. Details are on my website or you can get it on Amazon in paperback, e-reader and hardback editions.

Assertive people generally have excellent emotional intelligence and high levels of self-esteem and self-confidence. They are generally highly emotionally resilient.

If you discover, or more importantly, admit to yourself you are definitely one of the difficult types then you may need to work especially hard on reshaping your influencing style before you begin to see beneficial results in your interactions with others. As a supervisor, manager or leader you need to be as assertive as possible in order to influence others and guide your teams successfully.

If you are not behaving assertively what chance does your team have?

You might even consider working with a professional coach if a perceived lack of assertiveness is something you need to deal with first.

In summary, it is one hundred percent possible to deal assertively with all of the difficult types described in this guide and many more besides and I encourage you to start practising today and practising often.

In addition to being generally assertive, for each difficult type listed in this guide I will provide one or two specific key tactics to apply and my reasons for so doing.

It will be a steep learning curve for some of you and you will of course make mistakes. Do we not all make mistakes when we are learning something new or is it just me once again? Now I never said it would be easy did I?

Chapter Action Points

Now you know more about what assertiveness actually is, how assertive do you rate yourself as a manager or supervisor?

Do you err on the side of passivity and generally let things go?

Do you become aggressive? If so, are you hostile or manipulative?

Do you look for the easy way out or the easy option?

Do you tend to do the right thing no matter how difficult?

What styles do the other managers at your level and above exhibit? Are you merely playing "monkey see, monkey do" because this is the way everyone works in your organisation or industry?

Do you not want to be different?

Ask your own manager or supervisor for some honest feedback on your influencing style and level of assertiveness? If you are the head person then ask a trusted friend or adviser. Ask someone or take a test. Do this as soon as possible in order to get a feel for where you are right now. If you do not know where you are, how can you set a course for where you want to be?

Revisit your difficult characters list and try assigning an influencing type to each person. Does this help you make more sense of what drives each person's interpersonal style and behaviour?

Again, keep hold of your list and we will revisit it in the next action point.

Chapter 6

Start as you mean to go on

When talked about what assertiveness actually is in an earlier chapter, I mentioned assertiveness requires assertive communication skills, assertive body language, confidence and the ability to communicate calmly without attacking or yielding unnecessarily to another person.

It is only fair for me to expand a little on these requirements for you as a supervisor or manager in order to give you a fighting chance of success.

Here are some guiding principles and strategies you might like to consider adopting. These approaches will help you develop and succeed as an assertive supervisor and manager.

- Always protect yourself first so you can help and protect others. This idea is covered more fully in the next chapter so make sure you take a good look at this.

- Always make your managerial position and stance clear and transparent. State it up front and state it often.

Continually inform your team and colleagues what you believe in and what your standards are regarding interpersonal communication, personal behaviour and the equitable treatment of other staff and colleagues. Clearly state your belief in and adherence to HR and organisational policies on bullying, dishonesty and any other employee relations topics you feel strongly about. State you will always be fair and impartial and no exceptions will be allowed. If you have a zero tolerance policy on certain things then let the people around you know this.

- If you are clear and open upfront then anyone in your new team or department who wants to improve their behaviour towards others can do so. It is bad form to punish people for past deeds so do not spring any surprises on them. If you have been there for a while and are only now starting to introduce new ethical and behavioural standards and guidelines then the same rule applies; pick a start date, inform everyone and start the new regimen from there.

- Always and only act or respond to things you have observed yourself. You should not censure anyone based on hearsay or gossip. If someone comes to you with an informal complaint you cannot act solely on this. You must investigate and make your own observations. If someone comes to you with a formal complaint about someone else on your watch then you must obviously adhere to and follow your organisational HR guidelines and escalate it as appropriate.

- It is always best to start with the belief the difficult person may well be totally unaware of the effects of their behaviour. Inform them of what you have observed and the effects created by their behaviour and allow them reasonable time to take corrective actions. Follow-up to ensure the issues have been resolved. Provide practical assistance and/or coaching if it deemed appropriate. If they prove unable or unwilling to change their ways then you can proceed along the most appropriate disciplinary route within your remit or within organisational policy guidelines.

- Make sure you walk the walk. Lead by example and demonstrate consistency and fairness in all your dealings with staff and colleagues. This way people will know what you say matches what you do. You will have integrity. You will gain kudos and respect and you will be well on your way to being not just a good manager but a potentially first class leader.

Here are some general characteristics of assertive communication and assertive body language which you can use to get started and develop your assertiveness as a manager. This is not an exhaustive list of course as we are all different and will likely be assertive in different ways. It will however give you a good start and I will add more specific tips and strategies in later sections.

Use a firm, relaxed and fluent vocal style. Maintain a mid-range tone and situation appropriate volume whilst speaking at a steady even pace which allows you as much clarity and diction as possible. This is to minimise the chance of being misheard or misunderstood. Reduce hesitations and your use of distracting filler words, e.g. ummm, ahhh, you know, basically, etc., to a minimum. This increases your perceived authority and confidence.

When you speak use statements which are short, emphatic and right to the point. E.g. "I would like to…" or "I want you to…" Ensure you make clear distinctions between statements of fact and opinions. E.g. "I have observed…" rather than "I have heard..." Talk about your feelings and emotions without blaming the other person. E.g. Use "I feel annoyed when you do not consult me," rather than "Not being consulted by you makes me annoyed." Involve others in a collaborative solution focused approach. E.g. "What do you think about this plan?"

Listening well is a wonderful skill for anyone to develop but it is essential if you want to be a top-class people manager. Learn to listen actively with your body as well as your ears and you will get more from all your interactions with others. Make direct eye contact, lean in when the other person is talking, smile and nod frequently and make appropriate facial gestures as the other person talks. I will cover listening skills more fully in another volume in this series but feel free to check out the many on-line resources available to you.

To be assertive maintain an upright yet relaxed and balanced posture. Keep a non-threatening distance from the other person. Do not be a space-invader as this can also be seen as dominant or aggressive non-verbal behaviour. Use open non-threatening hand gestures and ensure your facial expressions match well with your emotion, your words and your speaking tone. Pay attention to specific areas such as your jaw and your eyes. Do not clench your jaw as this can indicate stress and aggression; keep your jaw relaxed. Keep your eyes lightly focused and do not stare at the other person as this might be misconstrued as aggressive. Try not to blink too much either as this can be perceived as nervous or submissive.

Note when you are growing as a person and a professional by developing more assertiveness can lead to people who preferred your passivity trying to hold you back or sabotaging your efforts. Be on your guard for such people and beware their tactics.

Developing assertiveness is not easy if you are not used to it but stick with the practice and application. Try to find someone you know to be assertive and copy their verbal and non-verbal communication styles. Practice in front of a mirror or record yourself. Work on your practice with a trusted friend or two. Work with a coach if you have one. I am still learning and developing myself every day. Life is a work in progress after all so stick with it.

I also know from personal experience it can be scary at first and it can be scary each time you encounter an unfamiliar situation or influencing style but the payoff for you and your staff can be huge.

As a last general comment you may be rightly wondering how you can spot potential issues with difficult people if they are not immediately obvious to you. Great question.

As the manager of a team, and in the absence of anyone speaking directly to you, one of the ways you might be aware of problems is by looking for sudden changes in the performance of your staff. As a good manager I would hope you take a keen and frequent interest in the performance levels of the team as a whole and of the individuals within the team.

This method is not fool proof of course as any number of factors can cause a performance drop in an otherwise great employee. The following scenarios however should activate your problem detection antenna and encourage you to take a closer look at the situation for possible personality issues:

- If a new member joins your team and a previously high calibre employee takes a rapid performance dive

- If someone who has performed well elsewhere joins your team and their performance drops off markedly and rapidly

- If a team member shows a distinct and uncharacteristic change of personality or attitude when around a particular individual or individuals

- Unusual cliques or gossip groups spring up when they were not there before or certain individuals appear to be excluded from or avoid groups they were previously a part of

Be an observant manager. If you know what your team looks like when it performs well then you will know there is a good chance something is up when you see marked changes.

Chapter Action Points

Are there any guiding principles you would like to add to my list? You are a unique individual so I would encourage you to adapt everything you read in these pages to suit your own beliefs, values and circumstances.

How many of the general characteristics of assertive verbal and non-verbal communication do you excel in already?

Which areas could you benefit from including improving or enhancing?

Pay particular attention to some of the characteristics of the difficult influencing types when you read them to see if you exhibit them yourself. If you do then you know what to do.

Modelling excellence is a great way to develop any new skill or technique. Find someone you particularly admire for their assertiveness and start apply their language patterns and behaviour to your own. Before long you will find yourself becoming more assertive and in your own unique style.

By the way, if you have never been on the receiving end of

bullying (lucky you) and you do not really know what all the fuss is about, try talking to someone who has been bullied or someone who has had badly bullied staff.

You may well be surprised just how much misery and damage bullying of any sort can cause.

Do not put up with it on your watch.

Chapter 7

Protect yourself so you can help and protect others

Before we go any further and as something of a reality check let us examine what the real world of business can be like.

I am assuming you are reading this book because you quite rightly want to be the best supervisor, manager and ultimately leader you can possibly be. You wish to adopt the principled stance of applying assertiveness in all your managerial interactions even if it means someone getting dismissed as a result. Making the decision to live by your convictions and stick to your guns come hell or high water takes real courage. This is indeed laudable on your part.

Without wanting to sound negative in any way I want to inform you principles can sometimes be extremely expensive. Principles can be expensive in terms of energy, time and money. Principles can even be career limiting or ending if you directly challenge or defy the wrong people or groups.

I generally adhere to a personal philosophy which, amongst other things, encompasses realism, pragmatism and utilitarianism. I have an approach which could be summed up as, "Does it work, will it do any good and will it benefit the majority?" I am actually self-employed as I write this so I already know my philosophy fits in with my current organisational culture and behaviour. I am not able to know your personal philosophy or situation of course but you do. If your values and beliefs are important to you must ask yourself whether they are compatible with the organisation you are a part of or not?

I recommend, as a minimum, you check and confirm the following three things are in place in both your organisational culture and your organisational HR system to make sure you do not suffer unnecessarily for having the courage of your convictions.

- Is there a clear culture of management and staff being encouraged, empowered and supported to do the right thing in your organisation?

- Will you get genuine back-up and support from other managers around you and your superiors if you do take a principled stand against any problem individuals within the organisation?

- Does the organisation have robust and fair HR policies and strong HR management in place which will give you the policy and HR support you need to usefully manage and control problematic staff?

If these are not in place you may be wise to take great care in planning how you will proceed with some of the people management options available to you. Even when the organisation as a whole espouses the good things listed above bear in mind some powerful individuals may still take a different position. What an organisation says it does and what it actually does are not always the same thing.

For example, consider the following questions:

- Are the necessary disciplinary procedures for what you are trying to do already laid out and agreed with staff and management?

- If you fairly and rightly put someone on a written warning or use any other disciplinary tactic will HR back you if the employee complains to higher management?

- If there is an attitude of cronyism and "who you know not what you know" prevalent then how will you be able to effectively manage people if they simply run off to their protector and you get warned off or worse?

- Will your staff or whole team get treated unfairly as a result of your actions being seen as "rocking the boat" by other managers?

Think about it. If the leadership and management in general have a hostile-aggressive or manipulative-aggressive style will you really be able to stand as a lone guardian of all things right and good?

I am not trying to put you off here but if you do not have your eyes open and you do not have a good grasp of the cultural and political norms in the organisation you are in and you directly challenge or defy them then you could find yourself in a deeply dispiriting and lonely place. There are many bad managers and bad managements out there so do not end up isolated and swinging in the wind through lack of basic planning or simple naivety. It is not a great place to be.

A more roundabout and possibly long-term approach may be a far better bet for you and the sustainable future of your career.

Instead of openly challenging or defying the status quo as a lone voice in the wilderness you may have to consider taking a more diplomatic and politically minded approach. You may have to pick your battles. You will not do your team any good if you are isolated and marginalised by opposing forces intent on limiting your effectiveness as an always do the right thing manager.

Seek your own support base at higher levels in the organisation. Work hard to change the system from within before you need to use it in anger. Gain multi-stakeholder support for your proposals and take a step by step approach to changing the organisational culture and policies. Good managers can make already poor managers look much worse so tread carefully and if possible try to take your peers with you. Clearly define and demonstrate the beneficial results your changes will offer compared to keeping things as they are and help them make the necessary changes. You will need to become an influential, politically astute and patient change agent.

Apart from your interpersonal and political acumen, the success of all the above tactics will also depend on available time scale and your relative position and power within an organisation.

Wow! Being a manager is not easy and being a stand-up always do the right thing manager is even harder.

You may even decide, having taken a long hard look at where you are and where you want to be, the organisation you are in is not a good fit for you. You may choose to move on to a position where you will be able to maximise your skills and do the most good.

No person is an island. We all need support and an environment we can flourish in so make sure you know the lie of the land. You have to protect and help yourself before you can protect and help others.

With the reality check caveat in place let us crack on and look at the influencing types in more detail.

Chapter Action Points

If you have not already done so, take some time and carefully establish the influencing style map of your organisation. Draw it out if it helps.

What is the stated organisational culture?

How does the stated culture compare to what really goes on? Do they just talk the talk or do they walk the walk?

How confident do you feel about the level and quality of back-up you will receive as a manager when trying to do the right thing?

Do you know where your real support lies? You may find help, support and back-up in some surprising places if you look hard enough.

Are you fully appraised of and familiar with your organisations HR policies relating to staff conduct and discipline? If not then you know what to do.

Do the right thing but first make sure you protect yourself so you can confidently help and protect others.

Chapter 8

The hostile-aggressive influencing style

Hostile-aggressive behaviour is often demonstrated when someone is domineering, pushy, self-centred or overly self-promoting.

Extremely hostile-aggressive individuals may be abusive, threatening and authoritarian. Their non-verbal communication may take the form of staring, glaring, frowning, finger pointing or other angry postures, gestures and movements toward others.

Hostile-aggressive behaviour does not always manifest in tantrums and rage. People can be hostile in quiet and calculated ways. They may resort to hidden one to one bullying or threats with the promise of dire reprisals if the situation is revealed. When they are fully covert operators they may be more usefully considered as hostile-manipulative types which will be covered in the next main chapter.

Hostile-aggressive people almost always try to communicate an impression of superiority and show disrespect to the people they interact with. Taken to the extreme, hostile-aggressive people are all too often outright open bullies. Their aggression is often the result of poor emotional intelligence and low levels of self-control. At first glance it might seem the aggressive types have ultra-high self-esteem but in reality the opposite is almost always true. They create an artificially high opinion of themselves and their superiority to everyone around them then, using the idea of attack being their best form of defence, they defend this false superiority at all costs with their aggressive tactics.

The hostile-aggressive generally does not much care who they upset as long as they get their way and as a result they can leave emotional devastation in their wake.

Whilst they may benefit from a feeling of power and control, as they coerce people into doing their bidding, it all comes with a hefty price tag in terms of enemies made, increased paranoia and rock-bottom self-esteem.

Openly hostile-aggressive people give many people in management their greatest cause for concern. When someone attacks you physically or verbally it can easily trigger your fight or flight response. It scares you. When this happens you lose objectivity and you think with far less clarity and logic than you normally would.

Being hostile-aggressive in response leads to pointless confrontation. Responding with passivity makes their life much easier and yours much harder. You could of course try being passive-aggressive and get them back slyly later but hey, do you really want to be such a person?

Of the three difficult types we will discuss, the hostile aggressive types are actually the least disruptive overall. They are often easier to identify. In the short-term they can be a real pain but because they are obvious and generally out in the open the decision to begin managing, or even avoiding them in some cases, is almost always an easier one to make.

As I hope you will appreciate by now, being assertive is the way to go as a manager of such people.

The Big Bad Bully

Description:

The Big Bad Bully uses various forms of hostile-aggression in order to intimidate others into compliance or allegiance. The Big Bad Bully might use anger, open or covert threats of failure or reprisal, blackmail, ridicule, guilt and/or shame. The Big Bad Bully will essentially use whatever tactic they can to get what they want. The Big Bad Bully has no worries about arguing or embarrassing others to achieve their ends. We are going to examine the openly hostile type here but be aware they can also be completely subversive (manipulative-aggressive) and harder to identify. This passive-aggressive version will be covered in the following main chapter.

The Big Bad Bully can also be something of a manipulative politician and a player of mind-games and they can often be incredibly charismatic with people when they need to be.

You will find The Big Bad Bully is a hypocrite as well; they will not be able to tolerate their own tactics when they are used against them. The Big Bad Bully will not hesitate to rant with open rage and extreme hostility if they believe it necessary to achieve their goals and this is the trait which makes them so easy to identify.

Make no mistake, if not properly controlled or dealt with, The Big Bad Bully and their many clones are dangerous to the morale and mental well-being of both you and the staff on your team or in your department.

Note some people may be overly ambitious and results driven and may use a lot of the tactics a Big Bad Bully might use but may be genuinely unaware they are causing so much misery. The may well assume everyone else is as thick skinned as they are.

Characteristics and underlying issues:

A Big Bad Bully rarely likes to work alone and often have a posse of acolytes around them. Having this group of adherents will bolster the bully's ego. For confederates they either seek people who hate confrontation, are generally fearful and compliant and who are essentially passive or they team up with passive-aggressive types who feel stronger and bolder as a result of the association. Bullies are generally great judges of character and tend to use any information gained about someone against them whenever possible.

If you will not join them or support them and especially if you stand up to them then you are their enemy; a simplistic black and white approach. Bullies are people with low self-esteem and poor self-image who seek to make themselves feel better by making others feel worse. Bullies are odious sad small-minded people who can cause a lot of misery.

Beneficial approaches as a manager:

The Big Bad Bully and others like them are often considered a manager's worst nightmare. You have to deal with them assertively.

I always recommend a zero-tolerance approach. Too many managers ignore bullies and bullying behaviour and hope it simply goes away. It does not. Set your boundaries early on and stick to them. Shine a light on their activities and stand your moral ground resolutely; show them you will not be backing down any time soon.

The first trick is to identify their tactics as they can cover their tracks well. Make sure you observe their bullying behaviour yourself and keep a record of what you have observed. When you confront them the meeting can go a number of ways.

In my experience many bullies, when assertively confronted by management, act as if they are the injured party and they can often appear as nice as pie. This is a front and you should stay firmly to your assertive approach which is based on your self-observed evidence. They may also become aggressive and abusive toward you but this merely confirms your observations. You may of course wish to have a second party with you in all your meetings to counter this possibility. They may also be genuinely surprised and shocked if they are unaware of the negative effects of their behaviour and if so they will be keen to correct it themselves. Now you can make your judgement call on how to proceed.

The real big bad bully will not like any of this assertiveness on your part one little bit and to them you will be public enemy number one. This can be lonely and dispiriting if they have been there a while and are entrenched and supported from above so make sure you have high reserves of emotional resilience before embarking on this course of action. In time, others will see your stand for the good thing it is and they will join you. Even the most entrenched and supported bully will eventually become isolated and will likely leave or request a transfer once their support dissolves and their cover is entirely blown.

Here's the bottom line. The negative behaviour they exhibit must stop one way or another. You are being assertive on behalf of your team. The bully will not get what they want of course but you remain assertive because you do not get aggressive or submissive yourself; you simply state that the negative behaviours as observed must cease immediately or you will be forced to escalate the matter. They may ask for help, such as coaching or mentoring for example, and if you believe it to be worthwhile then by all means help them. The final outcome is all down to them.

You will have grown as a manager and people will respect your integrity for taking a principled stand and effective action.

The Angry Diva

Description:

The Angry Diva is someone who wants to be the centre of attention all the time and always get what they want. The word Diva implies a female bias but it is just an expression. Men are just as likely to be Angry Divas as women.

Whatever the gender, in their world it is all about them and woe betide anyone who thinks or says differently. Many organisations have people like this at different levels and if you are really unfortunate they are sometimes even in charge.

Characteristics and underlying issues:

The Angry Diva can be arrogant, self-opinionated, always expecting praise and plaudits and often highly annoying to deal with. The Angry Diva is prone to tantrums and hissy fits and it is all about narcissism (if it is really extreme they may even have a personality disorder in this regard) and egomania with these people. They often feel and act as if the world and other people exist solely for them and they care little for the feelings and thoughts of others.

They have likely had success before with using their tantrums, much the same as a baby might, and have gotten so used to using this strategy they may struggle to influence people in any other way. Lazy or passive managers in their past have backed down and let them get away with it; enabling their hostile-aggressive behaviours. You now have to deal with it.

The annoyance they cause their co-workers may well become outright dislike if not handled well. They are hard individuals to manage and can create a toxic atmosphere and generate low morale if left unchecked.

To add to your difficulties as a manager they can also be charismatic and even well-liked between the times they act out their diva like behaviours but they are always seeking control over and the compliance of others. This can be to perhaps get an easy life or possibly to achieve certain results which they believe need to be achieved.

The behaviour styles as described could push them towards the passive-aggressive category but I have left them in the hostile aggressive because generally their control seeking and ego-centric behaviour is direct and overt.

Note they may also be unaware of their behaviour. As I mentioned earlier they are much like small children who learn crying can get something good like food or cuddles so they repeat the behaviour until it becomes a habitual or default influencing approach. It is entirely possible no one has ever confronted them with it or forced them to learn to change their ways.

Beneficial approaches as a manager:

The Angry Diva is often not actually doing anything maliciously wrong other than ranting on and generally getting people's backs up. They do this in order to get what they want.

Rather than simply confronting them and encouraging them to change their ways, which is a perfectly good approach by the way, I recommend trying make full and good use of the positive skills they do have.

This may be a controversial approach but you often catch more flies with honey than vinegar so it is worth a go. To potentially get the best from them, and in the process minimise their impact on others in the department, I recommend you take on the role as flatterer in chief and sell them on why they are needed and how the project work you want them working on will benefit them. This will appeal to their centre of attention ego.

Do not actually go ahead and give them any special treatment, rather let them think they are getting special treatment. The "special" projects they then get must have two cast-iron requirements attached which they must stick to in order to get the task - do not rock the boat and do not lord it over anyone else. I recommend making them sign something to this effect or confirming their compliance in an email. If they do have one of their rants or hissy fits ensure you take them away from others immediately and let them get it out of their system. Do not interact with them when they are in full rant mode; only re-engage with them when they have calmed down. You can then remind them you had an agreement and encourage them to stick to it or else. If they continue to refuse to play ball then go back to the fully assertive shape up or ship out approach. They had their chances after all .

The Know It All

Description:

There is nothing you or anyone else can tell The Know It All. In their opinion they have seen it all and done it all. There is no room for personal growth in their world but plenty of scope for it in other people.

The Know It All believes they can do or say no wrong but they will be extremely efficient and keen to point out where you and everyone else went wrong of course.

We have all met a version of The Know It All and they can be hard to be around, especially when you are forced to manage them, work on a project with them or participate in a small team of which they are a part.

Characteristics and underlying issues:

There is nothing inherently wrong with someone being a Know It All and they are not necessarily doing anything with malicious intent. They are often extremely good at their jobs and they often possess a great deal and depth of valuable information and skills. Despite this knowledge, you may still find it hard to maintain your cool as your frustration mounts.

The problems generally occur when you want to move forward with something new or innovative and The Know It All is able, via their position or expert skills, to block you and your ideas. It is not a personal attack on you or even your idea itself. The problem is not even a lack of curiosity; they often have plenty of curiosity. No, the problem is they feel duty bound or even compelled to attack or shoot down anything which they have not come with themselves. They are almost an intellectual equivalent of the Angry Diva.

They are in the hostile-aggressive camp due to the fact they are not shy about voicing their opinion or openly embarrassing other people in order to get their point across or establish the correctness of their position.

The Know It All type actually have super-high self-esteem and a super-solid self-image. What they almost always lack is the empathy and social/emotional intelligence to see how their behaviour affects those around them. They like pursuing their own ideas but they do not like to entertain your or anyone else's ideas.

Beneficial approaches as a manager:

Ideally you need to get the Know It All on side and make full use of them as a great resource. There are several workable approaches you could take to do this depending on your own personality and the time you have available.

You could try the old "let them think it was their idea" approach to get them on side. This may take some clever use of influencing language and some personal pride swallowing but does work quite well.

You could also learn about the topic so deeply you earn their respect as a know it all of equal stature but this could take a great deal of time and effort and they may get even more defensive and entrenched as a result. They might see you as competition.

Another alternative is looking to get them on board as a mentor but they would still have to feel you were worthy of their help. They really can be frustrating people.

It is rarely an ideal world so one last option, and it is the one which will probably work best for you in most cases, is to quickly decide the whole thing is a complete waste of your valuable time and energy and simply neutralise their power over you by working right around them. Give them projects or research tasks which are real and necessary but ensure they work on their own with tight deadlines and regular progress milestones. Keep them away from other people on your team unless contact or interaction is absolutely necessary. This strategy will work best of course by taking an assertive stance at all times when dealing with them and letting them know clearly who is in charge without being pushy or using bullying tactics.

I will freely admit the last option probably does not represent the highest moral position you could take but as a manager you have the whole team to think of and you do have to show results at the end of the day. Did I not already mention I was a pragmatist?

Chapter Action Points

Get out your difficult list again.

Are you able to assign the influencing type of hostile-aggressive to anyone on the list?

Are you able to match anyone on your list with the three specific examples I have given?

What sort of assertive approach might you try in order to manage or deal with these people?

Try scripting one or more approaches and run them by a trusted friend, colleague or adviser before working with them live in a one to one meeting with any of your people.

What sort of policy or HR options do you have at your disposal?

Keep your list to hand as we move on.

Chapter 9

The hostile-manipulative influencing style

Hostile-manipulative or passive-aggressive influencing behaviour results when a person is neither open nor considerate of others.

Whereas hostile-aggressive influencing types are open and direct, passive-aggressive individuals find far subtler, more subversive and more insidious ways to express or convey their feelings and reactions. They seem to go out of their way to secretly undermine other people rather than build themselves up.

Passive-aggressive types have low self-esteem and low empathy so they feel bad even when they are being nasty or demeaning to others. They are however, just like the hostile-aggressive types, good at reading other people and their emotional states and then "pushing their buttons;" this is definitely something to be aware of when you are dealing with them. Passive-aggressive personalities tend to adopt an "I lose you lose" approach in their lives.

They can be toxic people to deal with in any situation.

To add to the negativity and problems they cause, they are not always easy to spot because they often say things are okay when in reality they are not. They almost always appear collected and emotionally together on the surface as they hide their own low-level feelings way down deep.

A classic sign of this personality type is when they do things to sabotage or undermine the work, reputation or performance of co-workers or managers.

For example, a passive-aggressive manager may start to quietly exclude an unsatisfactory employee from crucial activities as a way of encouraging them to seek another job, rather than talking directly.

A passive-aggressive worker who is unhappy at the promotion of a colleague might start a gossip or smear campaign against them rather than be open and honest about their true feelings.

A passive-aggressive team member of any specific type can be a big drain on team and individual morale and, due to their clandestine approach, the situation can go on far longer than it necessarily should and can therefore create a few co-worker casualties on the way.

The first and essential thing to do when dealing with all hostile-manipulative types is to metaphorically drag them into the light. They will not crumble into dust like movie vampires but they do not like being visible and being seen by others for what they really are.

Almost without exception they know exactly what they are doing so be extremely wary and sceptical if they express surprise and sorrow when finally exposed and confronted. This will likely be just another method of manipulation on their part and as a manager you should have none of it.

Once again, being assertive is the way to go.

The Sniper

Description:

The Sniper is a strange character who inhabits the shadowy hinterland of the bullying world. The Sniper is not yet an outright overtly hostile bully like The Big Bad Bully but they will emerge to dip their toe into the murky waters of bullying by making nasty or sarcastic comments or ridiculing others before retreating quickly back into the shadows.

As I mentioned previously, the Big Bad Bully types often have an entourage of confederates or acolytes and many of these will be Sniper types who often feel they gain a measure of boldness from the perceived protection the association gives them.

The Sniper can be turned back to a righteous path with support and encouragement but if their hurtful and undermining behaviour is left unchecked they could become a more fully fledged bully or even a Svengali type which you will read about later.

Characteristics and underlying issues:

We are again looking at low self-esteem and extremely low self-confidence here. You will hopefully observe this is a common feature with all passive-aggressive types.

The will take pot shots at people they feel are unable to fight back. When someone is down they will be there to make them feel worse. The instant hit of superiority seems to energise them and, if it is also considered funny by other team members, they also benefit a little from the feeling of comradeship no matter the cost to the victim.

The Sniper's behaviour may only be rated by many managers as a low-grade form of bullying at worst but it is still bullying nonetheless. For the victim of any bullying activity it is no consolation to hear the bullying is considered low-level; perspective is everything.

To make matters worse The Sniper can often be seen as funny by some other managers and team members who are not on the receiving end of their barbs but this is no excuse for you as a stand-up assertive manager to turn a blind eye and allow it to continue.

The Sniper is a hypocrite like many passive-aggressive types. They react badly to anyone else sniping at them. This can be a good confirmatory sign if you are struggling to identify this type of behaviour.

Beneficial approaches as a manager:

Take a zero tolerance approach to all bullying activity on your watch from minute one and you will educate the people around you about what they can expect from you.

This will discourage bullies from operating anywhere near you or your team and it will encourage the rest of your team to respect and support you.

As with the other passive-aggressive types your most beneficial approach is to shine a light on the Sniper's activity and bring them, metaphorically at least, kicking and screaming out of the shadows where they normally operate. They will have nowhere to hide and will therefore have to cease and desist.

Whenever you hear them deliver a barbed comment or put down make sure you assertively challenge their statements, ask them to repeat them out loud for everyone's benefit and incisively question their statements so they will have no options but to be more open and direct with people. Allow them the chance to alter their behaviour themselves.

As a manager you can turn this behaviour round by working more closely with them and helping them build their own self-esteem and emotional resilience.

If they continue to exhibit the Sniper tendency then of course you should collect all the self-observed evidence you need and have the assertive cease and desist conversation first.

If necessary you can escalate the matter as per your organisational HR policy for all incidents of bullying.

The Guilt Tripper

Description:

The Guilt Tripper is the person who never lets people forget the bad treatment they believe they have had at the hands of bosses and workmates. They never let facts get in the way of a good story of course so although their moaning may have some kernel of truth they will happily exaggerate and embellish. Take their stories with a big pinch of salt.

They blame everyone but themselves for their perceived misfortunes and never miss an opportunity to tell anyone unfortunate enough or daft enough to listen of their woe-filled tales.

If you do not give them a particular task or project they want they will moan on and on about how you "did the dirty on them" or "stitched them up" and generally held them back.

Colleagues will get the same treatment if they are felt to have contributed to this heinous act.

They never seem to worry they might have failed to make the cut due to simple lack of merit or some other valid reason. No, it was an unfair act directed specifically and callously at them and no one else.

Like other passive-aggressive types they are adept at recognising and pushing the emotional buttons of others and guilt is a strong emotional button for most of us. They look for people who might either believe or support them or who might easily cave in to their bullying manipulative tactics. If you can smell the acrid stench of burning martyr it will likely be The Guilt Tripper.

Characteristics and underlying issues:

The Guilt Tripper is firmly in the passive-aggressive section because unlike The Mighty Moaner who moans all the time, The Guilt Tripper moans with specific intention. They, like the other passive-aggressive types, have poor self-esteem and low self-confidence. Although they are often ambitious and talented, they also often keenly suffer from the fear of failure and taking personal responsibility for their own lives. They blame the world for their failure and as a result they have little personal power.

They are also often just plain lazy and will be looking to avoid work through laying on the guilt rather than just getting on with it.

The Guilt Tripper will try to influence decisions with their trademark guilt trip techniques in order to make people who do not know them too well feel bad enough to grant them what they want. Passive people who do know them well will grant their wishes just to avoid the moaning and grief.

Whatever approach gets them what they want it is all fine with The Guilt Tripper.

At some stage in the past The Guilt Tripper may have had some outstanding success with their methods and now, like a baby who has learnt crying get cuddles or food, they keep doing it.

The Guilt Tripper either does not know how to change tack or has simply come to like getting ahead with little merit.

Beneficial approaches as a manager:

Assertiveness is once again key here. As a manager it is up to you to remain in control and keep your cool. Guilt is indeed a powerful emotion so do not collapse in the face of the onslaught of woe and misery.

Giving in simply reinforces their negative behaviour for the next time. You certainly should not feel guilt for any past events you had no control over. Even if you make a genuine mistake, once a sincere apology is given and appropriate correction occurs consider the matter at an end and move on. Offer to help them develop and grow as a valued employee but also make it clear to them you will not put up with their guilt tripping nonsense and if you hear them doing it in future you will class it as malicious gossip and therefore a bullying offence.

Take a zero tolerance approach with this type of thing.

Once they realise and acknowledge you are not about to roll over they will likely give up or even try to move on to fresh pastures. To continue with no easy results takes effort and inherently lazy people do not use effort if they do not get easy results.

The Malicious Gossip

Description:

I am sure we have all met a gossip such as The Malicious Gossip. They are the person who always seem to have a titbit of salacious, detrimental or outright scandalous information about someone or something they absolutely have to share - this is just between you and me of course.

Characteristics and underlying issues:

The Malicious Gossip is different from someone who merely talks or chatters a lot.

The Malicious Gossip likes to feel as if they know a secret about someone or something and cannot wait to share it with an enthusiastic listener. The big issue is with the fact The Malicious Gossip only seems to like negative information or information which is detrimental to someone else; it is of no importance to them whether the information is true or not.

What makes them an extremely pernicious form of bully is the fact they also specifically try to target their listener in order to achieve maximum grief for the target of the gossip.

They may have a particular personal grievance, real or perceived, with a colleague or manager but rather than openly deal with it they start a targeted smear campaign with their gossip. They may also just continue and expand gossip passed on from others as a general way to build themselves up by bringing others down. Either way they are poisonous, pathetic and generally nasty individuals who should be dealt with quickly and firmly.

Like the Guilt Tripper, they are also ones who never let real facts get in the way of a good story. They exhibits truly classic passive-aggressive behaviour. Due to their own low self-esteem and lack of self-confidence The Malicious Gossip likes to feel important and in control by virtue of their "special information" and knowledge.

They can often feel like they are fitting in as a result of their "entertaining" snippets. Many people on your team may also unwittingly encourage them by listening to the gossip and doing nothing to prevent it.

If challenged at any time, The Malicious Gossip will hide behind a "Well everyone else is saying it so do not shoot the messenger" approach and deny they are in fact the origin of the problem.

Beneficial approaches as a manager:

Low level office gossip is hard to completely eradicate so ensure transparent communication and information is available whenever possible and definitely avoid joining in with or sanctioning any of it yourself.

As a manager, if you hear about anyone spreading hurtful or malicious gossip you should first try to get some self-observed or heard evidence then directly challenge them with it. Remember a Malicious Gossip may not be above using gossip to implicate other people so always check the facts yourself. If what you do uncover yourself is bad enough then escalate things immediately as per company policy. If it is not yet so bad it still needs dealing with quickly and effectively and I recommend doing the initial assertive work behind closed doors. Inform them in no uncertain terms they are clearly and openly exhibiting bullying behaviour and now must they cease and desist. Feel free to issue dire warnings of future consequences. Tell them they are on your radar from now on. If it happens again you are then in a fully justifiable position to escalate proceedings. Demonstrate your resolve and do not back down.

Broadcast a clear and consistent message stating bullying via malicious gossip or indeed any other means will not be tolerated.

The Big Negative

Description:

The Big Negative sees the negative side of everything. If all The Big Negatives in the world got together and created a team slogan it would be on the theme of "We told you it wouldn't work."

The Big Negative has a negative response for every idea, suggestion or request put to them.

In extreme cases even the things The Big Negative has self-generated will be seen as only leading to disaster. The Big Negative can dampen enthusiasm and destroy team morale faster than anything else I know of.

Big Negative types are the poster children of despair and futility.

Characteristics and underlying issues:

The Big Negative is distrustful of all things management. Anything which challenges the status quo or threatens to introduce change is to be challenged, avoided or ignored. Management represents change to them. Because they fear failure they cling obstinately and vociferously to what they know but deep down there is often more to it. Ironically and confusingly they may actually fear success more. This is because when people or teams succeed they are expected to repeat the process. This will inevitably lead to failure at some point.

The Big Negative tries to avoid this success/failure rollercoaster by never starting anything or only starting it with the stated caveat it will fail anyway. Good grief!!

Now it may be true some Big Negatives are simply lazy and trying to avoid work in many cases they do genuinely care quite a bit about the team and the organisation and in a strange way are actually trying to be helpful. Preventing failure by not starting anything new is their way of doing this. A case of "If it ain't broke don't risk fixing it" so to speak.

The Big Negative is also generally not the kind who will actively sabotage projects but you may well find them in a Big Bad Bully posse as this may give them a feeling of more influence. Neutralising them early on or even supporting and encouraging them back on side and working positively with the rest of the team represents a great result for you as a manager.

Trying to directly get them to think positively and encouraging them to be upbeat will be met with huge resistance and even more negativity. The trick here is to get creative.

Beneficial approaches as a manager:

There are many approaches open to you as a manager. As mentioned the direct approach will generally yield poor results so more indirect approaches are necessary. These indirect approaches still have to be delivered assertively by you in order to work as intended. The key thing is to give them free rein and let them be as negative as they want to be. The trick for you is not to show their negativity has any emotional impact on you. This lessens the impact of negativity as an influencing technique.

Some extreme Big Negatives are what is known as mismatchers. Mismatchers are almost hard-wired to take an opposite stance to things. You might use this to your advantage with careful use of creative yet still fully assertive language.

An interesting technique, which often works with mismatchers, is to take their stated negativity even further by amplifying it then using their mismatching tendency against them.

For example, if they say a particular situation is bad, nod vigorously in agreement then point out even more dire outcomes and thank them for helping you out. It may seem counter-intuitive but this may well serve to get them to move to a positive defence of the idea just so they can mismatch you.

As another example, if you want them to carry out a particular task for you, start by telling them they will be unable to do it and ask them for suggestions about who else would be best. They will likely argue positively they can do it because they simply cannot help it. Reluctantly give in to their demands to do the job for you. Ensure you seek a strong commitment of intent from them preferably in an email. Is this manipulative on your part? Absolutely. They however are the passive-aggressive one in our scenario so it is merely a case of using their own traits against them. It is worth a shot.

Another useful approach is to acknowledge your appreciation of their good intention in pointing out potential pitfalls in your plan then make it clear to them the door is open for them to contribute more ideas for improving the project or process plan. This takes the success or nothing pressure off them and they may well take you up on it. They can often be a useful and valuable resource for you and your team despite their negativity so do not bypass them or marginalise them unnecessarily.

If they never change or even get worse despite your best efforts then you must consider the team as a whole and look for a suitable way to move them somewhere else where they will be happier. Perhaps within the organisation or possibly in the wider world of gainful employment.

Being assertive with yourself and trusting in your own decision making is often one of the most difficult thing any new manager can do. Making the hard decisions takes courage but those decisions generally yield the best long-term results.

The Countdown Kid

Description:

People nearing retirement in any organisation can be forgiven for winding down a little. They are bowing out gracefully with their heads held high. They might cheerfully and helpfully pass on their knowledge and experience to bring on their replacement before they go. Whatever they do they certainly do not prevent anyone else from getting on with their work or become a disruptive influence. It is human nature to slow down eventually and their thoughts will be on their coming new life phase. If they have given sterling service and continue to contribute to the end then who can blame them for not punching it out at the rate they once might have.

The Countdown Kid on the other hand is a person who is near to retirement but instead of going out gracefully and with class, is looking to work their ticket and play the organisational system for all it is worth.

At best they might be doing the barest minimum they can do to get by knowing you can apparently do little about it.

At worst they might be seeking to try and force the organisation into paying them redundancy, an early retirement deal or some other thing they feel is available and which will yield them more than mere retirement. They do not care who they have to annoy or disrupt to get it.

They are a common feature of many modern, especially large, organisations and in large part the organisations themselves have created the many opportunities for these people to play the system through overly-complex HR policies and poorly thought out historically created employment packages. Add to this new rules and regulations in HR and employment law and it is clear to see the fertile ground such people confidently operate in.

Characteristics and underlying issues:

The Countdown Kid is at odds with the organisation itself and not necessarily their department, colleagues or even you as their manager. The organisational policies often mean it appears cheaper to let them play their games until retirement. Redundancy can be expensive especially if the person has been there a long time. It becomes a battle of wits and wills and a grand contest to see who holds their nerve the longest.

The Countdown Kid tries to be as disruptive and useless as they can in order to coast in or be given a big pay out redundancy package whilst seeking to avoid any financially disastrous disciplinary dismissal. The organisation simply waits them out for the cheaper natural retirement option.

The issue for you as a manager and your staff is the fallout created by this contest.

The Countdown Kid can often appear to be the nicest person in the world on a personal level but the path they have chosen often means they will not hesitate to use or take advantage of anyone and everyone to get what they want. This is why they are solidly in the manipulative-aggressive category.

The Countdown Kid needs to appear busy and productive in order to try and avoid any disciplinary action. In order to waste time whilst looking busy they will often attend and extend every meeting they can, talk to any colleague polite enough to put up them for as long as they can, attend any training event they possibly can no matter how irrelevant and join any internal committee or focus group they can to burn up those minutes and hours.

They will often think nothing of taking strategic sick days or even sick weeks depending on what they feel they can get away with within company and statutory policy.

The fallout from this for you and your staff can be high.

The Countdown Kid does not or will not carry their fair share of the departmental load so others have to shoulder the burden. They still take up head count so cannot be replaced until they finally go.

They think they know all the rules and regulations so their self-confidence and self-esteem is high. They feel clever, untouchable and invincible. It is something like a game to them and they can often become addicted to the rush and thrill of it.

Using any pretence they can think of they will happily involve other staff in their time wasting activities. They are literally stealing valuable staff time which is in short supply and which has to be recovered or made up by someone.

The Countdown Kid is a toxic employee who can create misery and disruption around them in order to achieve their goal of the easy life or easy money big payoff.

The rest of your staff, and more than likely your own management as well, will feel justifiably annoyed and will look to you to sort things out. If you do not then the Countdown Kid could make you another victim of their grand scheme.

Beneficial approaches as a manager:

If you try and work with them to encourage them to change you will actually be helping them to waste time. Your staff will only get more annoyed the longer you delay taking effective action with this person.

I believe there is only one realistic approach for you as a manager and this is to assertively play a game of your own. I recommend you force them to be a productive employee or assist them out the door via the organisational disciplinary route.

Make sure you have all the information you need about the company's disciplinary procedure so you do not drop yourself or anyone else in it. Talk to your HR expert if necessary before you initiate any tactics or strategies.

I recommend you get creative and use the same systems they employ against them.

Select or devise a project which is beneficial to the organisation but not critical. Make this a project which is entirely suitable as a solo project. It might need interaction with others but it should be a project which could be completed by any competent individual possessing the right skills and knowledge. Take care to ensure all the elements of this project are within the skill set, knowledge range and ability of The Countdown Kid so you do not risk any accusations of constructive dismissal.

Set up clearly defined yet achievable SMART performance standards and fair measurable criteria. Install clear reporting milestones and the expected but reasonable outcomes at each stage. Set up regular short meetings to check on progress.

Here is the really important bit. Make The Countdown Kid solely responsible for this project and, apart from the routine tasks and meeting attendance required of any employee, remove all other workload and meetings from their schedule to allow them full ability to complete the new and eminently reasonable project.

The Countdown Kid will be well aware you have manoeuvred them into a corner and a number of things could happen as a result of this knowledge about your move.

The Countdown Kid can refuse to take the project on and you can now consider initiating a disciplinary approach based on this open refusal of a reasonable work request. This is a good result for you, your staff and the organisation.

They could get on with it and fail to deliver whereupon you can again consider initiating disciplinary sanctions. Another potentially good result for you, your staff and the organisation.

They could knuckle down and complete the project in a satisfactory manner and this is definitely a great result for you, your staff and the organisation. If required why not assign a similar project straight away and get more good results.

The last option may be when they choose to go on long-term sick leave. Any claims against or by the company will be taken up by HR. At this point The Countdown Kid is not disrupting your team anymore and you could even employ a replacement due to the long-term sickness issue. Another good outcome for you, your staff and in time the organisation.

Assertively managing difficult staff can require courage and a willingness to make some tough decisions and take the harder road.

The Poker Face

Description:

The Poker Face is the one who shuts you out. The one who blanks you. They try to get at people by deliberately closing down, giving nothing away and taking no obvious part in things.

In my experience this is the kind of passive-aggressive approach a small child might use. The adult is behaving like a small child. Despite all this, it can a powerful way of getting attention from others.

Their behaviour can be highly disruptive and energy sapping for a group and for you as a manager it can be extremely annoying and downright dispiriting.

Characteristics and underlying issues:

In reality there could be any number of reasons why The Poker Face is silent and this can make it tricky for a manager or colleague to develop an approach to overcoming it.

For example, it could be for a short period of time whilst they internally process some private personal trauma or significant professional upheaval. This could mean simply allowing them some time and space.

It could be linked with a current organisational activity or a specific set of conditions. It could be because they simply do not like you or one of their colleagues for some reason.

Another alternative may well be to do with the possibility they are poor communicators or extremely shy when dealing with management or others in authority. Their use of the silent approach as therefore a defensive measure.

Interestingly they may not be acting in a passive-aggressive mode at all. They may simply be completely unaware of the effect they are having on others as a result of their sullen, silent and passive-aggressive behaviour. Tactfully highlighting this or allowing them opportunities to change their approach may yield excellent results.

Beneficial approaches as a manager:

Identifying this influencing type will take some careful observation on your part. Do they blank you personally in an effort to influence outcomes or are they generally quiet with all managers? How well do they get on with other members of the team? Are they particularly quiet with the more boisterous or outgoing members of the team or management? Are they genuinely shy or are they manipulative?

If you conclude they are blanking you personally in order to gain some advantage over you or others then they are likely to be a manipulative Poker Face type and you should deal with them accordingly.
In my experience the best solution with this type is to give them no indication their behaviour is even noticeable let alone effective. I do not mean you should blank them in return but rather carry on as if nothing at all has happened.

Their communication style will be part of the front so I recommend you only ask open style questions which require more than a grunt or a yes/no response. Leave a lot space for their answers and make encouraging body language signals as you would with anyone you are actively listening to. If this makes them feel uncomfortable it is quite simply tough, do not forget the fact they started it.

Assertively assign them tasks and request confirmation of compliance via email. If they then fail to perform you are building up the evidence you may need if things escalate further down the line.

If you do feel the need to assertively challenge their behaviour I recommend taking the emphasis away from them and you and point out the negative impact this is having or will have on their friends and workmates. This may be just enough to shift them.

Be aware if you directly engage with and openly lock horns with the Poker Face they may turn in extremis into a Malicious Gossip with you as the target and they may well seek to become part of a Big Bad Bully posse if one is available. As ever, behave assertively, tread carefully, act consistently, treat everyone fairly and remain patient in order to get the best results for all concerned.

One last useful tactic I would recommend is to build in time-delimited clauses whenever you deliver requests and/or instructions to them.

For example, "Your response and input on this matter is highly valued. As you already know, there will be a severe impact on the ability of production to complete the order if no clear decision on this matter is made by the team. Therefore, if we do not hear from you by five o'clock on Tuesday evening we will assume you are in full agreement with the majority opinion of the escalation team and a final binding decision will be made then. I look forward to hearing from you."

They now have a reason they have to respond for the benefit of the team and nothing to moan about if they do not. Time-delimited material also gives you further ammunition and evidence if things worsen and the behaviour of The Poker Face needs addressing more seriously.

The Control Freak

Description:

The Control Freak is a perfectionist and as such is unwilling to and often almost incapable of delegating work to others. Even if they are capable of it they are often unwilling to do it. If The Control Freak does manage to delegate, or is forced to delegate, then they will try to micro-manage to such an extent they may as well have done it themselves anyway.

The Control Freak is consistently controlling with everyone they encounter. They cannot help themselves and will reveal their tendency despite any efforts to keep it hidden. The Control Freak is therefore relatively easy to identify and their behaviour can be extremely domineering at times (The Control Freak could well have been placed in the hostile-aggressive section).

Having The Control Freak on your team or, usually worse, having The Control Freak as your boss, can be a motivational sinkhole; morale can plummet.

To an experienced confident worker the Control Freak can be an annoying colleague but imagine how an inexperienced new starter, who is eager to please, could have their morale dropped into the basement by the constant put downs and interference a zealous Control Freak can generate. Not good.

Characteristics and underlying issues:

The control freak is fundamentally a perfectionist at heart and therefore has an underlying mistrust in the ability of others to do the same task to the same high standard as they can.

The reality is they are often highly skilled at what they do and the blocking tactics they exhibit in order to keep their tasks and projects make many managers give up and allow them their control. You will agree I hope this is not the assertive approach you aspire to.

They may well have deep feelings around lack of control in certain areas of their lives. These areas are usually the by now familiar self-esteem, self-confidence and overall emotional intelligence. The Control Freak will try and make up for these deficiencies by exerting control the things they do feel they have some real control over; tasks and co-workers activity.

It is again entirely possible the Control Freak is genuinely unaware of the effect of their behaviour. Control Freakery is based on perfectionism which can be a tough nut to crack. You can try working with them on it or get in specialist external coaches but only if they genuinely want to reform. You cannot change anyone directly remember.

Here is the bottom line, The Control Freak sincerely believes no one in the world can do as good a job as they can and they do not care who knows it.

Beneficial approaches as a manager:

Perfectionist Control Freaks on your team are often a nuisance and can indeed lower morale if left unchecked. Make sure you observe their controlling behaviour yourself and do not rely on hearsay or second-hand report. As I mentioned above, you will not be able to change their perfectionist traits directly, only they can choose to do this, but I do recommend using their traits to your advantage whilst limiting their interaction with other team members.

Give them work which needs to be as accurate as possible but make sure you carefully monitor deadlines. Get signed or emailed agreement with them for commitment and accountability reasons as well as for evidence if required later.

Give them valuable solo tasks and provide them with specific measurable outcomes and process/task directions and they will produce good work for you.

Here is the thing, assertively lay down the law and make sure they do not interfere with other team members. Assertively set distinct work boundaries from the start and, perhaps most importantly, make it abundantly clear to the other members of your team they must report any potential out of remit interference from the Control Freak directly to you.

Steer The Control Freak away from actively participating or joining project teams as anything other than a specialist for the detailed work which they will deliver in spades.

If the Control Freak is looking to reform they will benefit from and appreciate the new arrangement.

However, if The Control Freak is a full on deliberately passive-aggressive type they will feel too constrained by your knowledge of them and your control.

They will not like it one bit and may well move on at the earliest opportunity. Either way the result is good for you and your team.

The Control Freak can be hard to manage but with a bit of planning and rigid guidelines they can be used to full advantage and cause minimum team grief.

The Filter

Description:

The Filter is an interesting influencing type. It has a number of variations. I have chosen to put it in the passive-aggressive category here because people who exhibit and embrace the behaviours and mindsets of The Filter are often doing it for deliberate, calculated and specific personal reasons.

The filter tends to try and influence their world through information control. Depending on their position within an organisation they will filter and prevent certain information from passing up or down the line whilst allowing other information through. This is in an effort to manipulate the actions of others or to control the information others have to work with.

For example, a certain manager might withhold certain items of information from staff in order to control how they process the remaining information in order to feel they have more control over their staff. The same manager might also filter bad news or complaints from going further up the pipeline in order to appear more successful in the eyes of their superior.

As another example, consider an employee who withholds information from their manager to either cover up some problem they have created or to impede a colleague from succeeding in their task.

They are all deliberately filtering information for their own ends.

Note some information is organisationally restricted, for example via a non-disclosure agreement or in order to prevent insider trading, which is fine. The filter, however, chooses to withhold specific types of information for purely personal reasons in order to get ahead or impede others.

The Filter has a variant which I call The Secret Squirrel due to the fact they keep certain task related knowledge secret away from others. They may hope they can become the go to person for a particular task or type of project which will hopefully give them more kudos and also more security. This is ultimately detrimental to the organisation in the event they leave, retire or otherwise disappear and take the sometimes critical knowledge with them. Thankfully this is an old-fashioned view of the world and one which is fast disappearing in many modern organisations. Not fast enough in some cases.

The Secret Squirrel and Filter can also appear as variants of the passive Doormat type. The Doormat can often quietly take on small but mission critical tasks without telling anyone what they are doing. This will be as a genuine attempt to help out. They will often do these tasks so well everyone else forgets they are even doing them at all. The facts only come to light when the Doormat has had a meltdown or is off work for some other reason. They may also filter information up or down for many reasons and once again often with the best of intentions.

Characteristics and underlying issues:

The passive-aggressive Filter is basically driven by fear.

They may well have been brought up with the idea knowledge is power. Because they, like all passive-aggressive types, have ultra-low self-esteem and self-confidence they crave anything which can bolster them even if it is temporary and artificial. They may even have deep personal or work concerns and use the Filter or Secret Squirrel activity to maintain a fragile shell of normality to try and hold everything together.

Any feeling of power or normality created by the perceived control of information flow or the keeping of task secrets is always going to be a temporary feeling at best.

People talk and interact at and across all levels within a modern organisation and it never takes long before the power gained by the behaviours of the Filter or Secret Squirrel begin to wane. Their solution is to either work harder to control the same things or find new things to control.

If used exclusively the results generated by filtering or squirrelling activity are not usually enough for them so they may well exhibit Filter behaviour in conjunction with one or more additional passive-aggressive styles so be on your guard for this when looking to identify and control such types.

The people around such a personality type often have little respect for them and once the game is up and their behaviour becomes known people work around them or if possible avoid dealing with them at all. It can be difficult at first if you find yourself working under a manager who is a Filter but you can and will find ways around it.

Beneficial approaches as a manager:

If you have people on your team who are Filters or Secret Squirrels then it is well worth the effort of bringing them back into the fold to maximise the benefits of the real skills they do have.

As a manager you first need to make sure you are not a Filter or a Secret Squirrel yourself; deliberately or inadvertently. If you are then you need to sort it out. Seek coaching or support from a trusted friend, colleague or manager. If you are in the clear then you need to identify any offenders on your team and assertively deal with them.

Identifying this influencing type is relatively easy. Is the same person always doing the same task regularly and no one else seems to know how to do it? Do you hear information second-hand which they should have provided earlier? Does information which should flow on stop or change when it reaches them? Big signals.

I recommend collecting your evidence and assertively challenging them on their behaviour. Look for any root causes or concerns they may have and together you can work out a personal development plan to address the issues. Make sure they agree formally and state their commitment to the plan and deadlines.

If caught early enough there is always a way back. If they are wedded to their influencing technique and style then you may have no option but to escalate the matter. Collect your evidence, set your deadlines and accountabilities, review and analyse then hand-off to HR.

As the old saying goes, "You can lead a horse to water but you cannot make it drink."

The win-win outcome has to be for you, your team and your organisation.

The Svengali

Description:

The Svengali is a deliberate and covert controller of others. In my opinion the Svengali character represents the consummate passive-aggressive character; the one most people think of when they try to picture someone who is manipulative-aggressive. They operate in the shadows and their methods involve misdirection, clever language, coercion and smoke and mirrors.

They are, like most other passive-aggressive types, excellent readers of other people. The Svengali will carefully and deliberately choose their victim (often a highly passive type like The Doormat) then begin to work their malevolent influence. They are the ultimate expression of the Control Freak, Sniper and Bully types rolled into one. The Svengali will often appear as nice as pie to the other types which they cannot control and it is this ability which can make them hard to identify and challenge.

The Svengali can also be overly-ambitious in an effort to make up for their lack of self-esteem and will try to get there any way they can. The Svengali is a bully and can make their chosen victim's life a misery through verbal, behavioural and sometimes physical abuse in the workplace.

If you see someone's morale or performance take a nose dive and it is not a personal issue then you might be wise to suspect and keep an eye out for a Svengali type bully. They can ruin the working lives of several people before they are detected and often frequently move about career-wise to stay ahead of the game and avoid such recognition.

By the way, Svengali is actually a fictional Eastern European character in Trilby written by George Du Maurier in 1895. In the novel Svengali seduces, controls, dominates and exploits a young English girl called Trilby and makes her a famous singer.

Characteristics and underlying issues:

Many of the manipulative-aggressive behaviours we have looked at so far have had the common feature whereby the individual concerned could have been acting unaware of the effects they were having on others. Once they know the truth these particular individuals are often horrified to find out and can then work hard to turn things around.

The Svengali knows exactly what they are doing and why. For whatever reason there is a malicious intent to all they do in pursuit of their end goal.

The highly passive-aggressive Svengali type of control freak type will have super-low self-esteem and super-low self-confidence. They have little empathy but they will have a high degree of social intelligence. Many of them will likely have a feeling of powerlessness, inadequacy or lack of control somewhere in their lives but this is no reason to prey on and control others in an effort to make themselves feel better.

Usually they will try to remain in the shadows and control their victims covertly. They seek to undermine, bully and control others either for its own sake or to help them achieve some purpose they feel they cannot achieve on their own.

Beneficial approaches as a manager:

For the bullying and maliciously controlling Svengali types I again recommend a zero tolerance approach.

Most people deserve a second chance in my opinion an even the outright Big Bad Bully can mend their ways. No matter how good they are at their job The Svengali in my opinion is better dealt with by seeking dismissal.

They are toxic and can be a real menace if left to their own devices so whenever you personally observe behaviour consistent with this type of bullying manipulation, nip it in the bud. Invoke whatever HR anti-bullying policy measures you have and get rid of them as soon as you can.

If you have identified a victim of The Svengali or such a person has formally complained then work closely with HR try and try to protect them as best you can or potentially have them temporarily seconded to a safer environment whilst the issue is dealt with.

One big issue you may have to face is The Svengali may well have strong support higher up. They are great political animals and can often wield power and influence in high places. It is all part of the game with them. Tread carefully and patiently, gather your clear evidence and ensure you work entirely within policy and protocol limits when seeking to remove them. Use the system to protect yourself and your team at all times.

Assertive people look for a win-win. On this occasion the wins are for you and your team. Life is not always easy for managers and supervisors.

Constantly and consistently broadcast the message stating you adopt a zero tolerance attitude to bullying of any kind and ensure you live up to it.

If you allow bullying to happen it will happen.

Chapter Action Points

Get out your difficult list again.

Are you able to assign the influencing type of manipulative-aggressive to anyone on the list?

Are you able to match anyone on your list with any of the eight specific examples I have given?

Do some further research on line because the manipulative-aggressive influencing type overall has far too many varieties to effectively cover in one book. To confuse things even more people can even adopt more than one difficult style.

Generally speaking these types can be far more difficult to identify, especially for new managers, and even harder to challenge directly. Time and experience will help but generally speaking an indirect and carefully planned approach often works best.

What sort of assertive approaches, direct or indirect, might you try in order to manage or deal with these influencing types?

Again, try scripting one or more approaches and run them by a trusted friend, colleague or adviser before working with them live in a one to one meeting with any of your people.

What sort of policy or HR options do you have at your disposal for dealing with these types of difficult people?

Keep your list to hand as we move on to the last main type.

Chapter 10

The passive influencing style

Passive influencing behaviour is inhibited, suppresses personal feelings and seeks to avoid conflict.

Passive people often try too hard to please others. Their influencing style is based on giving away personal power. The passive person therefore ignores their own needs and feelings to try and satisfy the needs and feelings of others; as a result they can often experience feelings of low self-esteem, frustration and sometimes emotional withdrawal. They do not express their honest thoughts, beliefs or feelings. They can turn anger and other potentially negative feelings inward.

For the passive influencing type other people are almost always provided with more rights than they provide themselves.

Their verbal and non-verbal characteristics can include hesitancy when speaking and the use of long rambling disconnected sentences containing weak language such as "I might be wrong, I probably am in fact, but if you would not mind maybe..." or similar. Their voice is often soft, monotonous and quiet with their sentences often dropping away or tailing off into awkward silence. Their passive body language might include slouching and a gaze-averting downward looking head orientation. Passive people appear generally cowed and defensive with possible mismatches between facial gesture and real emotional state.

As a manager of people, you might be thinking of this as something of a dream scenario because the passive person should be easy to control but actually the reverse is true.

By being overly passive and indirect, communicating a message of inferiority and allowing the needs and rights of others to take preference over their own the passive influencing types often end up feeling like victims and this comes with the associated victim mentality and behaviour. Other people will often perceive them as victims and respond to them in like manner.

We have all encountered this extremely passive type I am sure and it is sometimes hard not to take advantage of their weak behaviour. Passive people tend to adopt an "I lose you win" approach to life.

This victim mentality can lead to poor overall performance, increased stress and even physical sickness for the passive individual.

In my experience passive types tend to need more managing at work and can often be a bigger long-term drain on group morale than the passive-aggressive and hostile-aggressive types.

Generally then, to get the best out of the passive types, you have to be extra assertive with them and be assertive for them as well.

The Doormat

Description:

The Doormat just cannot say no.

No request gets rejected in an effort to please anyone and everyone who asks them to do something. Does this make them somehow super-productive? Does this make them a dream employee? No way!

The Doormat is normally so over-subscribed and over-committed they end up pleasing no one. Doormats essentially and effectively educate those around them to take advantage of them.

Co-workers are often expected to take up any slack in order to keep the organisation, department or team in good standing. The grumbling will start and you will have to manage the fallout. This is all hugely ironic because the situation is often the direct result of the same co-workers taking advantage of The Doormat in the first place; all leading to the current overwork meltdown situation.

If you have a Doormat for a boss then are you in for a super-rough ride. They will take on too many tasks for the team, most of which cannot possibly be achieved, then to add insult to injury they will be too weak to defend the team against complaints about poor performance. A nightmare scenario.

The Doormat is almost always a lovely super-nice individual and everyone generally likes them but they can be a bully magnet, a definite target for The Svengali and a general disaster waiting to happen for their peers, staff and co-workers.

As I mentioned earlier in the section on The Filter, The Doormat can manifest certain other problematic traits. The

Doormat can often quietly take on small but mission critical tasks without telling anyone. This will be a genuine attempt to help out. They will often do these tasks so well everyone else forgets they are even doing them at all. The facts only come to light when the Doormat has a meltdown or is off work for some other reason. They may also filter critical information, up or down, which might upset someone often with the best of intentions or because they do not like conflict or do not want to upset anyone.

The road to hell is paved with good intentions.

Characteristics and underlying issues:

People who try too hard to please others do not do anyone any favours in the long run. They lack an ability or willingness to plan or prioritise and they do not think through the implications of what they are signing themselves or their staff up for.

They feel real fear about letting people down by refusing requests. If they refuse then they believe people will not like them and this will negatively impact their self-confidence. They already have low self-esteem and they desperately desire the approbation or approval of others.

The key thing for you as a manager is they really do mean well. The downsides to their well-meaning tactics and behaviour are potentially huge if you do not manage the situation assertively and effectively.

Beneficial approaches as a manager:

If you suspect you have a Doormat on your roster keep a close eye on their workload. Ensure you do not become part of the problem by adding to it.

Assertively Managing "Difficult" People

Sorting out the mess once an overload meltdown has occurred is dispiriting and time costly. The key here with managing The Doormat is to address the issues at the front end of the process.

Now I would not normally recommend micro-managing but here I believe it is essential. You must be assertive for them or assertive by proxy if you like. Set boundaries and guidelines and hold them accountable. Remember they can be dismissed for continual poor performance if it comes down to the wire so they have real skin in the game too.

Work with them in a manager/mentor role to help them improve their planning or, in extreme cases, you might consider having all work requests routed via you first.

Ensure you make it clear to the other people on your team any unauthorised work requests made to the individual concerned, or indeed any other potentially de-railing interference, will be frowned upon and assertively dealt with by you.

With an eye toward the back end of the process be assertive with the passive person and hold them fully accountable for any missed deadlines. Monitor deadlines and deliverables closely. Cut them no slack and do not do them any special favours or others in your team may become resentful.

Make sure you monitor and check for any unintentional or unreported Secret Squirrel or Filter activity which may represent an organisation destroying time-bomb ticking away right under your nose.

The Doormat may well turn things around themselves once they realise people like them better for actually refusing sometimes and completing the work they are supposed to complete. They may well see the solid results this assertive approach generates.

Turning a doormat around and watching them flourish as a result can be one of the most satisfying results you can get as an assertive manager.

The Silent One

Description:

At first glance you may wonder why The Silent One is in a list of difficult personality types. Continually quiet people are the ones you can forget about, right? Not really and for two reasons.

The first reason is The Silent One can be the one who puts a subtle dampener on the office vibe. The one who always sits away at lunch or hides in their office all day. Their work always gets done and it is always done well but nobody really engages with them and they never really engage with anyone else.

The true Silent One of course does not usually care about this. The true Silent One cares about preserving their space and solitude but is not actually sullen or aggressive about it.

The true Silent One is harmless in reality but their behaviour and general demeanour can be subtly disruptive for overall team harmony. Ignore this and simply treat them the same as everyone else.

Some people of course are simply shy. If such people try to engage then hopefully everyone in the team will be united in helping them bond and fit in. Your job as manager is to ensure this takes place when appropriate and no bullying or marginalising is taking place.

The second, and biggest, reason is you can become a problem yourself if you start obsessing.

Characteristics and underlying issues:

There may be any number of reasons why someone like The Silent One is quiet and there is little point speculating. As long as you are sure it through choice and they are not the victim of a Svengali or a Big Bad Bully or have some other personal issue which is making them quiet. You need to take the trouble to quietly and unobtrusively check these things out using your own observations and interpersonal skills.

If you are not careful about your approach you can also become a bit obsessive about actively trying to get them involved. You will get frustrated because The Silent One will almost always revert to their preferred quiet existence. Their style of behaviour is often a deliberate choice but it is rarely directed at anyone or anything specific. It is simply the way they prefer to interact (or more precisely not interact) with the world around them. It is therefore definitely in the passive section.

Do not automatically assume The Silent One is passive in a pleasing all Doormat kind of way (although they might well be of course) as this could be a mistake. Work may simply be something they have to get through to survive and if you or anyone else pushes too hard they may well surprise you with an angry outburst or two. The upside is at least an outburst would be more engaging and interesting than silence.

Beneficial approaches as a manager:

The reason the Silent One is in the list is not because they are difficult. It has more to do with people's desire to connect with them.

As a manager dedicated to developing more effective skills it is hard not to try and get everyone on your watch involved in the "we're all one big happy family" scenario. This can be a difficult desire to overcome but you must overcome it. If you keep pestering the Silent Ones you may be hovering near the harassment zone. There are more important battles to fight.

Take care not to become obsessed with trying to bring these quiet types out of their shell. The best way to manage them is to treat them the same as everyone else. Ensure everyone else does the same. When they feel the pressure to engage ease off they may actually choose to engage themselves so do not make a big fuss if they do; carry on as normal.

I also recommend giving them slight preference as the choice for any tasks which best suit their quiet style because you will get more from them this way. Acknowledge their value and contribution as a result. Do not take their lack of interaction as a personal insult; it is not.

As a caveat, the only time to feel there might be a personal problem between you and The Silent One is when they are only silent or sullen with you. Then they may well be a Poker Face type and you may need to alter your approach accordingly.

The Mighty Moaner

Description:

We have all met at least one of these characters in either our professional or personal lives. What a nightmare they can be. All they do is whine and moan day in and day out. They moan constantly. I believe if they had nothing to moan about, they would be moaning about having nothing to moan about.

They are a serious atmosphere drain. If you have got one or more Mighty Moaners on your team then you need to sort it out before everyone gets brought down.

To the Mighty Moaner everything is bad. Nothing can possibly have a positive outcome and nothing is, or will ever be, good enough for them.

They are markedly different from The Big Negative because they do not moan deliberately or specifically or take an opposite stance on purpose. What they do is simply moan about everything indiscriminately. They are wholly passive, pathetic and annoying.

The weight of the world is on their shoulders and boy are they going to make sure everyone around them hears about it.

Characteristics and underlying issues:

The Mighty Moaner is like a great big adult baby who has discovered crying gets them the attention they crave. Getting attention lets them feel important. They generally feel unimportant and helpless which indicates ultra-low self-esteem. Are you noticing a common thread in all these types yet?

The Mighty Moaner often does not appear to know what happiness is. They seem to gain no joy from life or work and they seem to live in perpetual misery; misery with themselves and the world around them. Misery as they say loves company so for The Mighty Moaner, creating conditions where others feel bad seem to be the only outcome which appears to make them remotely happy. They often give the impression they would moan on forever if no one stopped them.

Whatever event or situation got them started way back when there is no good reason I know of to let them carry on their continual moaning on your watch. If their experience is currently so bad then perhaps they would be happier moving elsewhere. If you they do want to go I suggest you assist them to smoothly transition away from the organisation.

If someone has had a recent upset or a situation has driven them to excessive moaning then it is entirely possible they are so wrapped up in their own thoughts they are unaware of the misery they are currently bringing to others around them. If, once it is made clear to them, they are keen to change then by all means work with them to achieve their stated goal.

For the habitual Mighty Moaner you really will have to do something about them so on this occasion I recommend a robust, direct and continuously assertive approach which they will find hard to ignore.

Beneficial approaches as a manager:

Deliberate and specific assertiveness is your key here.

You can potentially turn The Mighty Moaner around by keeping on top of some or all of the following ideas. If you do not turn them round at least you will reduce the effect on everyone else.

The key thing is to never let their moaning dampen your own spirit. Maintain high gumption and emotional resilience levels before dealing with them (also see my book The Resilient Professional).

Be forceful and assertive in all dealings with them. In meetings or conversations assertively force them to focus on solution or idea generation only. Interrupt them if necessary but do not let them deviate or backslide into negativity or you will be right back to square one.

Always talk in positive future-oriented terms and keep things focused on specifics; vagueness and lack of clarity leaves ambiguity which The Mighty Moaner loves to wallow in.

Interestingly, whilst it was potentially useful to agree with The Big Negative it is pointless trying to agree with The Mighty Moaner unless you want to end up moaning as well.

I recommend taking no actual position on anything they are currently moaning about. The only thing in my experience which a Mighty Moaner likes almost as much as moaning is a pseudo-debate which simply gives more for them to moan about. You will never change their mind directly. Definitely do not get drawn in to trying to solve anything for them as no solution will ever be good enough.

Always keep them reined in and focused on solutions and if they fail to play along then assertively end the conversation or subject topic and move on until they get the message.

Hopefully, other people on your team will see your approach yielding results and they may start to interact with more assertiveness. The Moaner will have two choices at this point. Get the message, change behaviour and remain as a valued member of the team or fail to get the message, carry on regardless and potentially face moving on to pastures new.

If they never do get the message then collect any necessary physically observed evidence you might need then offer them the chance to move on to pastures new where they might be happier and invite HR to join the party. This may make them shut up for a while at least.

If they do leave your team, your department or even your entire organisation it is still good news for all concerned including them.

A true win-win outcome.

Chapter Action Points

Get out your difficult list again.

Are you able to assign the influencing type of passive to anyone on your list?

Are you further able to match anyone on your list to one of the three specific examples I have given?

These passive types can be far more difficult to manage due to their passivity. If you are too challenging or assertive then they will simply retreat further into passivity and the situation worsens.

The need a firm hand and positive reinforcement. They can take up a lot of your time and energy resources but are often some of your most diligent and effective team resources when handled well.

What sort of assertive and positive approaches, direct or indirect, might you try in order to manage or deal with these people?

Again, try scripting one or more useful approaches and run them by a trusted friend, colleague or adviser before working with them live in a one to one meeting with any of your people.

These influencing types rarely require HR support but you could seek additional external coaching or training to accelerate desired change programs they elect to pursue? Never forget the potential for dismissal due to continual poor performance does also apply to passive types as well.

Is anyone difficult yet type unassigned left on your list? Are they actually a difficult employee at all?

Armed with your new knowledge how could you begin to put a plan of action together to understand, support, manage, neutralise or otherwise assertively deal with any additional difficult types for the benefit of yourself, the team and indeed the whole organisation.

Look again at your list and start to analyse, prioritise and plan your change program.

All in a day's work for the assertive manager.

Chapter 11

The workplace psychopath

So far I have identified and discussed fifteen distinct types of "difficult" personality you may encounter in your role as a manager. You will be able to spot these and use the suggested techniques to deal assertively with them. These types tend to manifest only one, and occasionally two or more, styles of difficult behaviour such as anger, rage, laziness, indolence, passivity, silence, superiority and many more besides but I would be remiss as an author on dealing with difficult workplace types if I did not mention one final personality you may encounter. I will provide some advice on how to best deal with or simply survive them. I refer to the type known as the workplace psychopath.

In fact, if you are currently dealing with a difficult person who defies your efforts at classifying due to too many different indicators you may well be dealing with a psychopath. Take extra care to look after yourself at this stage. Read the following and make a judgement call or even consider seeking advice from a trusted and more experienced mentor before proceeding. Also consider reading more books which are specifically focused on bullying and workplace psychopathy or explore the many on-line resources available if you wish to dig deeper into this topic.

What then is a workplace psychopath?

If we think of psychopaths at all we likely think of them as being like something out of a horror movie. An emotionless machine-like monster who inflicts pain, fear, misery and even death with no signs of remorse. All too sadly, these monsters really do exist and a good number of them are thankfully now in our prison systems. The chances of meeting this criminal type of psychopath are slim so hopefully you have had the good luck to avoid them. However, you may well have encountered a workplace psychopath or two in your time.

There are a trio of psychological traits and personality disorders which can be linked with problematic or even criminal behaviour. They are Machiavellianism, Narcissism and Pyschopathy. Together they are known as the Dark Triad.

- Machiavellianism is so named after the Italian diplomat Niccolo Machiavelli who, during the Renaissance, wrote a study in courtly intrigue and manipulation called The Prince. In modern times Machiavellianism is evidenced by someone with a duplicitous interpersonal style, a minimal regard for morality, and a keen focus on their own interests and personal gain.

- Narcissism is named after the Greek myth in which the youth Narcissus and fell in love with his own reflection after he rejected the advances of the nymph Echo. He turned into a flower which also bears his name. Workplace narcissists do not generally turn into flowers but they can be hugely problematic. Nowadays

Narcissism can be broadly defined as the pursuit of gratification and reward from vanity or an egotistic over-admiration of one's own attributes and abilities.

- Psychopathy, also synonymous with sociopathy, is an anti-social personality disorder (ASPD) and broadly typified by an attraction to power and control, persistent antisocial behavior, impaired or absent empathy and remorse, along with a forthright, dis-inhibited and highly egotistical approach to their lives and work.

There is somewhat of an overlap in the three dark triad measures and for your purposes as a new manager and I will refer to them from now on as a workplace psychopath because this is a term most people are familiar with. The exact pathology does not really matter, only the results of numerous issues combined in one person who you now work with or for.

Note that we can all at some time or another exhibit some of the above mentioned traits, we are only human after all, but when they are strongly evident in any one person it can be a real problem for those who have to work with or for them.

There are a number of standard and robust psychological tests which can be used to identify and quantify these traits but unsurprisingly, unless we are trained and active psychiatrists, we are not generally able to utilise these as we go about our daily lives. You cannot simply ask someone to fill in a questionnaire. We instead have to rely on building our knowledge and using or sensory awareness to spot them then we must rely on our skill and judgement to deal with or avoid them.

Now, you may have already identified that many of our difficult types can exhibit some of these three specific traits and in varying degrees. People who embrace all three dark triad traits and to a high degree are thankfully in the minority but the composite workplace psychopath is more common than we might suppose.

In everyday life there are varying estimates to be found but the average appears to settle on about one to two percent of the population who are nearer the high end of the measuring scale. This does not mean they will all become axe-murdering maniacs or serial killers or but they are there nonetheless.

In the business world it has been estimated that as many a three to four percent who test high on the negative traits. This might seem alarming until we consider for a moment that the traits mentioned above for the dark triad are also the traits which could propel certain people to the top of the corporate ladder. Ironically many workplace psychopaths are, and are seen as, very successful at their work especially in the arenas of politics, business and even high stakes sport. Many people, for example, see business virtue in those people who display and embrace these dark traits. It is a dog eat dog world out there after all they will say and it takes a strong will to get to the top. Perhaps this behaviour might be mitigated a bit if the people concerned could switch off the traits once they got to the top but this does not happen as once at the top they carry right on spreading their misery. They also create a swathe of devastation and misery through the organisational ranks whilst on their way up the greasy pole. They may very well be superficially charming and supremely confident but they will stop at nothing and stomp over anyone to get ahead and not feel one tiny bit of remorse or guilt.

Please note that you do not have to be a psychopath to successfully get to the top and lead any sort of organisation or department; at least ninety six percent of people in business are well-adjusted and normal individuals - phew! The problems start when you encounter one of the four percent. If you find yourself standing between them and their goals then you represent a real problem to them; one which they will be keen to deal with. Be on your guard.

Now with all the above in mind as you go happily about your managerial day, how exactly do you spot such a workplace psychopath?

One popular test, best administered by suitably qualified and experienced experts, commonly used to assess the presence of psychopathy in individuals is the Psychopathy Checklist - Revised (PCL-R). It was originally developed in the 1970s by Canadian psychologist Robert D. Hare.

The PCL-R comprises twenty elements and I have added short clarification statements after each:

1. Display glib and superficial charm - psychopaths often do very well at interviews and social gatherings
2. Exhibit grandiose (exaggeratedly high) estimation of self and abilities - they are big-headed and conceited
3. Show the need for stimulation - they get bored easily and often seek novel and stimulating activity
4. Engage in pathological lying - they care little for truth, lie often and lie with skill and ease
5. Are cunning and manipulative - they assume everyone around them is inferior and believe they can easily manipulate them
6. Displays a lack of remorse or guilt - they do not feel bad or guilty having done a bad thing
7. Evidence shallow affect - they display a lack of emotional response when a strong emotional response would normally be appropriate
8. They are callous and lack empathy - they simply do not care when bad things happen to others
9. Live a parasitic lifestyle - they generally prefer not to work too hard and find it "smarter" to take things from others

10. Poor behavioural and self-regulatory controls - they have poor emotional intelligence and can be excessive/obsessive as a result
11. Engage in promiscuous sexual behaviour - they like to put it about a bit
12. Have a history of early behavioural problems - they often have a history of cruelty toward others
13. They lack realistic long-term goals - they live very much in the now and prefer "crazy right now" over deferred gratification
14. Demonstrate high impulsivity - if they want it then they go for it with little thought about consequences
15. They display irresponsibility - doing the right thing is not high on their priority list
16. Show failure to accept responsibility for own actions - for them it is always someone else's fault
17. Have many short-term marital relationships - they are not big on commitment either and will repeatedly betray those who trust them
18. Have a history of juvenile delinquency - the psychopath starts young
19. Revocation of conditional release - when given second chances they tend to mess up again and again
20. Displays criminal versatility - they will do whatever it takes regardless because for them "rules are for suckers"

Please note the many trait crossovers within the dark triad group

By their very definition these people can be hard to identify. The workplace psychopath will also lie on a psychopathy spectrum ranging from mild to strong and this adds to the issue of identification.

As you have already read to this point by now, and hopefully followed the action points and completed the tasks, you will have a much better appreciation of personalities within your organisation note that you will also have a keener eye than most managers and leaders when it comes to spotting differences and problems.

In terms of psychopath spotting you should therefore be on the lookout for a cluster or combination of traits and behaviours based on the following three broad groups:

Interpersonal

> This area relates to a person's ability to deal with other people. The potential workplace psychopath will be superficially charming and highly self-confident when you first encounter them. Now this in itself is no reason to condemn anyone as many people possess such attributes but you may need to factor it in to the bigger picture. You may very well find yourself drawn to them as they can be very charismatic and even appear fun and easy going. Ideally they would be identified prior to being hired but, given their ability to turn on the charm, interviews are often a breeze for them. They are effective networkers and will often seek to build connection platforms in order to move up the corporate ladder with ever increasing velocity. They may not have a full range of emotional intelligence themselves but what they are often very good at is identifying reaction triggers and potential weakness in others then pushing the right buttons when they feel the need.

Affective

> This area relates to moods, feelings and attitudes. Whilst initially charming and likeable they will start to show more unpleasant traits with time and you in turn may notice more of these yourself. The potential workplace psychopath will display a marked lack of guilt or empathy.

Whenever they mess something up they will blame others. If they upset someone they simply will not care. You may not know anything about their home or private life, and I recommend you do not ask, but they often have a poor track record where relationships are concerned. They will often betray people close to them if it suits their objectives. They generally do not form deep attachments with anyone so you may notice this over time. That said, they may well indulge in some illicit sexual relations with their co-workers (hopefully out of working hours). Try not to get involved with them yourself as this is just asking for trouble.

Behavioural

The potential workplace psychopath is often a risk taker; either with their resources or the organisations resources. They display inadequate impulse control so be alert for displays of inappropriate emotion or language coupled with an all to ready willingness to flirt with danger. They are excitement junkies and hate to be bored. If you give them routine tasks they will always find ways to dump them on someone else or simply avoid them. They can fake trustworthiness very well and they are happy to dupe and coerce their colleagues and peers and they will frequently lie and cheat to achieve their ends. They can appear bold and dynamic but there is a fine line between this and recklessness. They will often exhibit a range of bullying tactics so be on your guard at all times.

Note that many of the traits mentioned above are exhibited by the difficult types we have encountered so far but not in such profusion. Add in elements from the other two dark triad types and you and your organisation have a potentially huge problem on your hands. As I said earlier, the workplace psychopath has to start somewhere and one or more of your leaders, peers, co-workers and staff may well be fully functional psychopaths looking to climb the tree at all costs.

Positively identifying a workplace psychopath can take time as you need to not only build up a clear picture but you need to be sure of your identification. You might consider quietly consulting a trusted colleague for their opinion on the person concerned or even put very gentle feelers out to your wider network to seek their opinions. A big, big caveat here. Do not overtly voice your concerns and seek confirmation but instead ask only for other people's general opinions of the person and add this into your overall mix. As we shall soon, it can be better not to put yourself directly in the firing line. The old saying that "Once you grab the tiger by the tail you had better hang on tight" is very apt. No one said being a manager was easy. When all is said and done you may miss the signs altogether and be aware you have one on the team only when it is far too late.

So now you have reasonable confidence you have identified a workplace psychopath within your immediate vicinity and possibly even under your authority as their manager or leader. Now what?

Be aware that it is not illegal to be a psychopath. Psychopaths can to do illegal and immoral things of course but merely being high on the scale is not enough to condemn someone. The very first thing to do therefore is refrain from accusing them of anything and trying to initiate dire proceedings against them. As you now possess valuable knowledge and when contemplating any potential conflict it is always a good idea to do so from a position of strength. I recommend you immediately take stock of your situation and ensure your defensive lines are properly established and fit for purpose.

Ensure you have a solid network of trusted confidantes and advisers. Preferably people who have no direct connections with the psychopath. Workplace psychopaths will often use a divide and conquer strategy to try and break down your normal communication routes. Make sure you have some strength in depth. Having some solid allies you can count on will pay dividends. You too can serve as their ally should you be needed.

Always be the best you can be at your work. Document all your achievements and keep scrupulous records. Keep them safe in a variety of locations as company records can and do get tampered with. This approach serves the purpose of protection in the event that the psychopath (especially if it your boss) turns their attention toward you. Even if you never have to lock horns with the psychopath your work and working habits will be improving and your team will also benefit; there is actually no downside here.

As an additional measure, start to document any openly hostile or aggressive behaviour as well as any indirect or covert behaviour exhibited by the suspect. You are not going to use this information for offensive purposes but it may prove very useful as a defensive tool later on if any conflict or harassment situations do occur. Being paranoid can definitely have its uses.

Now, because you have some forewarning of the situation I recommend spending as little time as possible engaging with the psychopath. Keep under their radar whenever you can. Limiting your exposure limits your chances of becoming involved in their games and intrigues. Note that this also means having no open discussion about them or their behaviour and making no direct accusations about them. Being a hero will do you little good and possibly much harm. Remember that these highly toxic people are expert at keeping out of trouble and using others to get what they want. You cannot change them as at the time of writing there is no known way of treating psychopathy other than isolation and removal.

There is only one surefire winning way to deal with a psychopath and that is do not deal with them at all. This would be my primary advice to you. Take a metaphorical run to the hills and avoid them like the plague.

If you do have to deal with them then perhaps some of the following information will be of use to you. Everybody and every situation is unique of course but I have summarised some broad brush general ways to deal with or at least survive a workplace psychopath.

If you happen to be their boss then I recommend firing them as soon as possible. Make sure you have the necessary ammunition and legal basis to do this but get it done as soon as possible. Does this sound harsh and/or cowardly to you? It is in fact a brave and highly assertive action. Be aware that they will not change and you cannot change them so just get rid of them the first chance you get or have HR do it for you. If you take the passive route and hope it all works out in the end then they will go on and create much misery for the people within your organisation.

If you have to deal with them because they are your boss or you work together in a tight team then remember the following:

It is a battle you are unlikely to win. Surviving is the name of the game here so engage with this goal in mind at all times

Always endeavour to be as emotionless and cool as possible. Do not play any of their games or fall for any of their fake charm. Try to remain cool and be neutral at all times. When communicating with them stick to facts, ask for specific examples to back up any jibes or attacks and always try to remain in safe territory. Remember, psychopaths prey on those whom they perceive as weak and they feed off the fear of others. By remaining completely neutral and demonstrating you are neither weak nor fearful they will likely bypass you and move on. If you appear as some sort of barrier or obstacle to them or they wish to benefit from your efforts and output in some way then they may escalate the conflict. This can get hairy and you may need to inform your higher management allies and/or your trusted HR contacts if you do come under direct attack. You may have to consider harassment charges and if your company does nothing to help you then for your own sake and sanity you must seriously consider leaving the organisation. No job is worth a life of misery. It may well become all about self-protection in this situation and good mental and physical health is more important than mere money. Bear in mind, you can always seek trusted legal advice for potential redress at a later date.

Whenever possible keep control of the situations where you have to engage with them. Do not engage with them on communication platforms, such as email, which favour divide and conquer techniques. Email allows them to easily involve others in their efforts to undermine them. Remember they are good at this kind of game. Unless you absolutely have to engage with them, I suggest ignoring them completely. Definitely ignore any overt or covert invitations to engage in any type of skirmish and treat them as the bear traps they surely are. If you have to engage with them do so on safe communication grounds and, better yet, in places with witnesses present who can be relied upon.

I recommend you plan ahead and create coping strategies if certain situations arise. The psychopath thrives on creating imbalance and confusion in others so being prepared will give you something of an edge and will make you far more resilient. Run a number of what if scenarios and consider the type of neutral response you might give or useful actions you might take. Always have at least a plan B, C & D in the back pocket. In fact, the more options you give yourself the better.

Try to limit your contact in order to prevent becoming involved in their games and machinations. If you are in the firing line then try to ensure you are never alone with them at any time. If you do find yourself in a one to one situation then stay as neutral and unperturbed as you can and keep any conversations away from you and turn it back to them whenever possible. This prevents them getting any additional leverage which they might use against you or against others. They are nasty people and they will use whoever they can and do whatever they feel it takes to achieve whatever twisted goal they have in their nasty minds.

One key thought to bear in mind is this. When all is said and done none of this is about you personally. By definition the psychopath has no feeling at all toward you or anyone else as an actual person with feelings and emotions. You have simply been unfortunate enough to be between them and something they wanted.

If you are not under such severe attack as to be looking for a new job or off on the sick with stress then try to remain patient and keep your nerve. Because of their intellect and upward drive the workplace psychopath will often move quickly toward the glory they seek or even move laterally in order to get a path to power. Either way you and your co-workers can breathe a sigh of relief, dust yourselves down and rebuild your working lives.

It may sound obvious of course but prevention is always better than cure so what can you do at an organisational level to keep these people at bay and prevent them being hired in the first place?

It is really a Human Resources (HR) issue but I will offer a few suggestions here which you may be able to apply or perhaps suggest to HR and the rest of the executive (hopefully psychopath free at this point) management team to help them create a more robust defensive process.

- Take care to exercise full due diligence. This is a critical point. Check references and do as much informal career history digging as you legally and morally can. Such due diligence can cost a bit more time and money during the hiring process but you will view it as a bargain if you do avoid a psychopath joining your organisation.

- Use multiple interview levels with similar "trip-wire" questions in each to check for inconsistencies. For example, consider asking them to relate their take on various tricky case study situations. Given that the typical workplace psychopath warms to superiors and is often rude to people they consider inferior, that is everyone else alongside or below them, you may get a few valuable red flag responses if you mix up the status level of the interviewers.

As ongoing good practice for organisations I suggest you create and foster an open and transparent organisational communication culture. Excellent communication routes both up and down coupled with a robust, anonymous and trusted employee suggestion system will keep a bright spotlight on serial offenders. Psychopaths do not generally like to operate in clear sight.

Maintain organisational awareness of and instruction on trust, ethics and integrity. Train your key supervisors, managers and leaders to be fully aware of, and on the lookout for, psychopathic behaviour patterns. Be an organisation which does the right thing and makes it easy for employees to do the right thing.

Emotional resilience is the ability to bounce back from negative emotional impacts. If you have to deal with any difficult people you will need as much emotional resilience as you can get. It is especially vital to build resilience before any contact with an office psychopath. If you would like to learn more about building emotional and mental resilience you could do a lot worse than buying and reading one of my other popular books which is entitled "The Resilient Professional." This is available on Amazon in a number of formats.

That is all I want to say on this topic. Once again I will point out that the odds are very much against you encountering a very strongly psychopathic co-worker or boss but the fact remains they are out there. Forewarned is forearmed so stay vigilant and take great care if you do encounter one. excel.

Chapter 12

Modelling excellence and learning from others

We all have to start somewhere and you will have made great progress by reading this book. Just buying the book shows you are keen to learn and grow.

We can all learn through trial and error. We can make mistakes which will be very painful but ultimately highly educational. It has been said that smart people learn from their mistakes. I maintain that even smarter people learn from the mistakes of others.

Being able to identify areas for personal growth then seeking out ways and means to create the personal growth is a sign of high emotional intelligence. To be successful in the life you choose to be successful in takes courage, patience and tenacity. It also takes an ability to see and take advantage of every opportunity which presents itself to you. You can and should take advantage of modelling excellence; either directly via mentoring or indirectly via personal observation and practice.

The following may appear to be an obvious statement but I will say it anyway. There will be people within your organisation and within your personal and professional networks who are good at the exact skills and approaches which you wish to improve in yourself. Why not tap into this resource to accelerate your learning and reduce the steepness of your learning curve. Learn from the results of their learning.

You could ask them directly for their help as a mentor or coach. Most people are flattered by such a request and will offer you some of their valuable time and knowledge. Always be prepared for them to say no. In fact, give them an easy out if they want it. Preserving the relationship is important. If they say yes then respect their time. Make copious notes and only ever ask pertinent and useful questions. React to their advice and apply it. Take care to see what success you have and credit them appropriately when others remark on your improved managerial skills. Not everyone works well with a mentor or coach so it will depend on personal choice. This is generally the fastest method of improving and if the stakes are high enough why not consider paying a professional coach to you get to where you need to be?

If you don't want to engage with someone directly on a mentoring or coaching level, you can also simply observe them in action so to speak. How do they speak to people? What physiology do they exhibit? What results do they get? Does their style appeal to you as one you would like to emulate? Well here is the good news. You can now try out their various tactics and approaches for yourself. When you next need to be assertive you can try out their language patterns and tone of voice or copy their physiology. If it works then keep it in your toolkit. If it does not then try something or someone else. It will be a work in progress and a work over which you have full control.

You could even look at people who are bad at being assertive and unfortunately you will likely find you have many examples to choose from. What are they not doing? What are they not saying? Do they make the situation worse? If you are exhibiting any of the same approaches or tactics then stop using them. Eliminate the bad and add the good.

These things can take time of course but persevere and you will get there.

There is nothing wrong with standing on the shoulders of giants. They stood on the shoulders of other giants at some stage. In the future people may well model your management and leadership approaches when they want to excel.

Chapter 13

Summary and your next steps

You have done it, you have reached the end of "Assertively Managing Difficult People" which is a part of my "The New Manager's Survive & Thrive Guides" series.

I hope you have found it stimulating, informative and, more importantly, useful to you as a new manager or supervisor.

We have looked specifically at "keeping your cool" and staying assertive whenever you are managing and dealing with difficult influencing style personality types and dealing assertively with the difficult situations they can create.

Everyone is different and confusingly we are all different in different ways and at different times. I never said it would be easy did I?

So remember, there are four main influencing styles: Assertive, hostile-aggressive, manipulative-aggressive and passive.

Assertiveness involves being completely clear and open about how you feel, what you needs and how it can be fairly achieved. This requires assertive communication skills, assertive body language, confidence and the ability to communicate calmly without directly attacking or yielding unnecessarily to another person. Assertiveness follows a basic win-win approach to life.

In my experience it is one hundred percent possible to deal assertively with all of the difficult types described in this guide and many more besides so start today, practice and begin to enjoy becoming the cool-headed professional who negotiates smoothly through all their interpersonal interactions no matter who they are with.

Everything in this guide is just that - guidance. The tips, techniques, tools and broad brush descriptions of people and personality types cannot cater for every eventuality. Get used to making your own value judgements on the effectiveness or applicability of the material in this book. Every situation you will face will be unique in some way and as your confidence, experience and options increase with time you will develop your own ways of working assertively and your personal style of assertive communication.

As a final note, always remember your role as a supervisor, manager or leader is to use your skills and the skills of your team to get the best results possible for your organisation. Using a rowing boat analogy may help illustrate this. You will ideally achieve this with everyone on board rowing the boat in the same direction and all benefiting from the shared resources and rewards. Some people will simply not get it and some people will not pull their weight on the oars. Some people will actively work against you and the rest of the crew. You are not there to rehabilitate lost souls and not everyone will make it to the end of the voyage. You may have to make some difficult decisions and cast off dead weight so the boat moves faster and/or more safely toward its destination. No one ever said managing and leading people was easy and I wish you well on your voyage.

If you want one to one help with any specific or personal issues which might be affecting your emotional intelligence, interpersonal communication or management experience then get in touch with me. You can contact me via my website at:

    www.andrewdpope.com

Keep in touch and maybe we will meet in person one day. I look forward to it.

Legal notice & general disclaimer

The author and publisher has striven to make the content as accurate as possible at the time of the creation of this book.

However, the author and publisher assume no responsibility for any errors, losses or omissions resulting from using the information provided in this e-book. By reading this book, you acknowledge you assume full responsibility for the use of any materials and information contained herein. Any perceived slights of specific persons, peoples or organisations are unintentional.

Under no circumstances will the author or publisher be held liable for any loss or damage caused by your use or reliance on information published herein or contained in any resources referenced in this book. This includes but is not limited to any websites, books, e-books or any other such materials. If you do not agree with these terms, you should not read this book.

In practical advice books, like anything else in life, there are no guarantees of success achieved. Readers are cautioned to rely on their own judgement regarding their individual circumstances and to act accordingly.

This book is not intended for use as a source of legal, business, accounting, medical or financial advice. All readers are therefore advised to seek the specific services of competent practitioners in these fields.

Unauthorised redistribution of this book is not allowed. Do not reprint or give away copies of this book. Instead, please invite your friends and colleagues to buy their own copy from the Amazon store. Thank you for respecting the hard work of the author and publisher.

Printed in Great Britain
by Amazon